D1625109

Grace-Filled Moments

The publisher and author are grateful to those publishers and others whose materials, whether in the public domain or protected by copyright laws and cited throughout, have been included in this volume, particularly in the Appendix. Other than sporadic conventional adaptations, minor modifications (primarily for stylistic consistency) have been made in a number of the excerpts incorporated in this book. Some of the Scripture verses used in this work are taken from the Catholic edition of the *Revised Standard Version Bible*, copyright © 1965 and 1966, and the *New Revised Standard Version Bible*, copyright © 1989 by the Division of Christian Education of the National Council of the Churches of Christ in the U.S.A., and are used by permission of the copyright holder; all rights reserved. Other Scripture citations are taken from *The Jerusalem Bible*, copyright © 1966, and *The New Jerusalem Bible*, copyright © 1985 by Darton, Longman & Todd, Ltd., and Doubleday & Company, Inc., a division of Random House, Inc., and are used by permission of the copyright holder; all rights reserved. Still others are from the *Douay-Rheims* or *Challoner-Rheims* edition of the Bible. Special thanks are extended to the following: the United States Catholic Conference, Inc. — Libreria Editrice Vaticana for the use of several excerpts from *The Catechism of the Catholic Church, Second Edition*, copyright © 1994, 1997; Sophia Institute Press, Manchester, New Hampshire, for permission to reprint material from *My Spirit Rejoices*, by Elisabeth Leseur, copyright © 1996 by Sophia Institute Press. Every reasonable effort has been made to determine copyright holders of excerpted materials. If any copyrighted materials have been inadvertently used in this work without proper credit being given in one form or another, please notify Our Sunday Visitor in writing so that future printings of this work may be corrected accordingly.

Our Sunday Visitor Publishing Division
Our Sunday Visitor, Inc.
200 Noll Plaza
Huntington, IN 46750

ISBN: 978-0-87973-899-0 (Inventory No. 899)
LCCCN: 00-140017

Cover design by Amanda Miller
Front cover photo by Shutterstock
Back cover photo by Erich Lessing/Art Resource, NY, of *The Virgin of the Host*, by Jean Auguste Dominique Ingres, Musée d'Orsay, Paris
Interior design by Sherri L. Hoffman

PRINTED IN THE UNITED STATES OF AMERICA

For my two daughters,

Jessica and Thea,

whose call is to carry the banner of truth, faith, and
authentic femininity into the Third Millennium.
May God bless you,
and all young women,
whose mission of spiritual motherhood is desperately
needed at this time in the history of mankind.
May the Blessed Virgin Mary intercede for you,
and may you model yourselves after her,
The Perfect Woman.

Contents

Acknowledgments

To set out to write a book is no light undertaking and in many ways it requires the common vision of numbers of people. I have been blessed to have many supporters in this project, as well as many who have shared the mission to help women experience the fullness of their femininity.

Thank you to Our Sunday Visitor Publishing for taking on this project with enthusiasm and zeal. And thank you also for permission to use the wonderful information provided in *Our Sunday Visitor's Encyclopedia of Catholic Doctrine* (edited by Russell Shaw). A special thank you to Michael Dubruiel, my editor, for your patience, understanding, helpful suggestions, and kind ways.

Thank you to Father Edmund Sylvia, C.S.C., theological consultant to *Grace-Filled Moments*, and my friend, for your insight, advice, and encouragement.

Thank you to Scepter Publishers, Inc., for permission to use the excerpts from *Our Moral Life in Christ* by Aurelio Fernandez and James Socias.

Thank you to Sophia Institute Press for giving me permission to use the many wonderful quotations of Elisabeth Leseur from her journal, *My Spirit Rejoices*.

Thank you to Servant Publications for giving me the opportunity to quote so extensively from my own book, *Full of Grace: Women and the Abundant Life*.

Thank you to those publishers in the Bibliography who are not mentioned above, from whose works a number of excerpts are used in this book.

Thank you to the staff of Living His Life Abundantly® International, Inc., for your support as I completed this project.

Thank you to my children, Jessica, Simon, and Thea, who have taught me so much about what it means to be "mother."

But, most especially, thank you to my husband, Anthony, whose patience, understanding, and generosity gave me the time, space, and love necessary to write *Grace-Filled Moments*. May God return your kindness to you one hundredfold. I love you with all of my heart.

If there are any errors or omissions in *Grace-Filled Moments*, they are completely my own.

Preface

Grace-Filled Moments is a response to the women who have asked me to prepare another book on authentic femininity. It has been both gratifying and humbling to see how the Lord has used *Full of Grace: Women and the Abundant Life* to encourage women in their gift of authentic femininity and their mission of spiritual motherhood. My fervent prayer is that *Grace-Filled Moments* will provide yet another opportunity for women to explore the gift of their gender and its spiritual call.

In this our day and time, the need for the gift of authentic femininity and its call to spiritual motherhood cannot be overestimated. Has there ever been a time in the history of man when so many forces have converged to threaten human life, family life, and spiritual life — all in the name of "enlightenment," "choice," "advancement," "science," and "technology"? I am reminded of the final words spoken to the women of the world at the close of the Second Vatican Council: "Reconcile men with life and above all, we beseech you, watch carefully over the future of our race. Hold back the hand of man, who, in a moment of folly, might attempt to destroy human civilization. . . . Women of the universe . . . you to whom life is entrusted at this grave moment in history, it is for you to save the peace of the world" (Pope Paul VI). These words are sobering and they issue a call to action to the women of the world, an action for which God has specifically chosen us.

Pope John Paul II has said that "in every age and in every country we find many 'perfect' women who . . . have shared in the Church's mission" and whose "witness and achievements have had a significant impact on the life of the Church as well as of society" (*On the Dignity and Vocation of Women*, § 27).

These "perfect" women have been women of faith, women of holiness, women committed to bring hope, healing, and life to the world through the fundamental call of their gender. They are "an incarnation of the feminine ideal" and serve as a light leading others to a deeper understanding of authentic femininity and the abundant life in Jesus Christ.

The names of these women are written in the annals of history — St. Teresa of Ávila, St. Thérèse of Lisieux, St. Catherine of Siena, St. Elizabeth Ann Seton, St. Edith Stein, to name a few — and their contributions to the Church and to society are legendary. To this day they continue to lead and to guide, to teach and to inspire, to comfort and to heal.

Someday, other women may find their names written alongside of these feminine giants of the faith: Mother Teresa of Calcutta, Elisabeth Leseur, Gertrud von le Fort, Dorothy Day, Alice Von Hildebrand, Jutta Burggraf — like the holy women who have preceded them, they too have heard God's call to transform the culture of the day through the call of spiritual motherhood. And they have responded, each in her own way. They, too, have served as beacons of light, modern-day heroines who show that dedication, self-sacrifice, and surrender to God yield an abundant and holy fruit.

Using the words of holy women, *Grace-Filled Moments* encourages women everywhere to be those "perfect" women in this, our day and time. To be women who enter into the fullness of their feminine call. To be women who "aid humanity in not falling," as the Second Vatican Council's closing message *To Women* points out. To be women who bear Jesus to the world through the gift of self-donation. To be women who make their own the words of the Perfect Woman, the Blessed Virgin Mary, "I am a handmaid of the Lord. Be it done unto me according to thy word."

This call is not a call for the fainthearted. It is a call for women of strength and vision, for women of hope and faith, for women who are willing to pour themselves out like a libation for the sake of saving souls. I hope you are one of these women. And I hope *Grace-Filled Moments* will inspire you in some small way to enter fully into the grace of authentic femininity and the call of spiritual motherhood. Let us promise to pray for one another as we seek to serve Him Who is Father, Son, and Holy Spirit.

How to Use *Grace-Filled Moments*

Grace-Filled Moments is a study guide that leads the reader into a time of prayerful meditation on the great gift of femininity. It can be used individually or in a group setting. Fifty-two meditations make it the perfect study to use throughout the year. The meditations can be presented one per week for a full year's study, two per week for a six-month study, three per week for a four-month study, or four per week for a three-month study. The truly ambitious may prefer to pray one meditation per day for fifty-two days. Each selection provides ample opportunity for deep reflection and prayer.

The selected meditations are structured around St. Edith Stein's description of the feminine soul. Each quality of the soul highlighted by the saint serves as a section heading and provides the central theme for each prayer meditation in that section. Note that each section states the theme and identifies a corresponding grace to pray for. The theme should be reviewed and the grace should be requested at the beginning of each prayer meditation. Most sections have seven prayer meditations.

The meditation features an inspirational quote from a spiritually great woman (and a few men, too!), a prayer to acquire the virtue or attribute presented in the quotation, a Scripture Passage for Meditation, and questions for reflection. The questions for reflection encourage the reader to explore the truths presented in light of her own life.

If *Grace-Filled Moments* is used in a group setting, the women should have reflected on and prayed through the quotation, prayer, Scripture passage, and questions prior to each group meeting. A facilitator should encourage each member to share her prayer experience of the meditations.

The group meeting is not meant to be a time of problem-solving, emotional or spiritual counseling, nor a gripe session. Rather, it is a time to discover how the Holy Spirit is mightily present in each woman's life. The members of the group must be receptive listeners who seek to "hear" the action of the Holy Spirit at work in the lives of their sister members. The facilitator should be sensitive to the dynamics of the group. Her role is to establish an open and respectful environment, to make sure each person has time to share, and to help ensure the confidentiality of the group.

How to Pray the Meditations in *Grace-Filled Moments*

Step One: **Compose yourself for your time of prayer.**

Prayer is a special time that we set aside to meet with God. It is often best to have a regular and consistent *time* and *place* for prayer. While this is not always possible, it contributes to consistency and helps to lessen distractions. Begin your prayer time by asking the Holy Spirit to illumine your mind, open your heart, and help you to be receptive to His movement within you. Because God is omnipresent, He is right there with you as you begin your time of prayer. Remind yourself of this reality and place yourself in His presence.

Step Two: **Review the theme for the meditation and pray for the grace.**

Go to the heading of the section. Review the theme and pray to receive the grace it identifies. These "graces" relate to aspects of our feminine identity, our relationship with God, and our call and mission in the world. A "grace" or "charism" is a gift given to us by the Father out of His abundant love for us. It cannot be earned or merited — it is freely given in God's perfect time. However, we can help ourselves to be disposed to receive the grace through daily prayer, frequent reception of the sacraments, and a holy and upright life.

Step Three: **Pray the quotation, prayer, and Scripture passage.**

Because of the inspirational and instructive nature of the selected quotations, they provide an excellent opportunity for meditation. Read the quotation slowly, not reasoning about it so much as pondering it in the heart. Let it slowly begin to take root in you. Read it a second time, aware of any words, phrases, or ideas that strike you or touch you. When this happens, stop and let the mystery unfold within you. Notice any feeling, emotion, or intuitive knowing. Let it develop in the inner recesses of your heart. Does it spark any memories, speak a word of instruction to you, or give you new insight? What may the Lord be saying to you through the quotation? Stay with the moment until it passes. This is mental prayer.

Repeat the same process with the prayer written for the meditation.

Do the same with the Scripture passage.

Step Four: **Answer the questions in the Daily Reflection.**

The questions offered in the Daily Reflection are in-depth and thorough. As a result, each meditation can offer several days of reflection. If this is the case, work through the question groupings one at a time, returning to questions for deeper consideration when necessary. If you are working through one meditation per day, review all of the questions, stopping at the one or ones that seem to strike your heart. Honestly and faithfully respond to the questions, searching for the answer beyond the answer. Our first impulse is often a reaction rather than an honest reflection. Let the light of the Holy Spirit reveal to you what may be hidden in your heart. Allow yourself to receive the impact of the reflection in the depths of your being. As St. Teresa of Ávila reminds us, there is no spiritual growth without self-knowledge.

Step Five: **Respond to God's action within you through a prayer.**

This prayer should take the form of a brief conversation. It should come from the heart and be a response to the interior activity of your prayer time. Often, it will take the form of thanksgiving. Sometimes it will be a prayer of repentance and contrition. It could be a prayer asking for more guidance or insight. It might also be a cry from deep within asking for God's healing mercies to descend upon you. The important aspect of this prayer is that you are aware of God's listening ear, lovingly attentive to your words.

Step Six: **Journal your insights.**

Record any insights, thoughts, inspirations, and movements in your heart that you experienced during your time of prayer. Some days you may have much to write. Other days there may be less. The important thing here is not quantity, but rather an opportunity to solidify and concretize the action of the Holy Spirit within you. You may wish to notate any question, thought, or movement that seems unresolved so that you may come back another time and submit it to the never-failing guidance of the Holy Spirit.

May these meditations serve to lead you into a deeper relationship with God as He reveals to you the great gift of your womanhood. May God bless you and may the abundant life of Jesus Christ be yours.

JOHNNETTE S. BENKOVIC
FEAST OF ST. THÉRÈSE OF LISIEUX
OCTOBER 1, 2000

Section One

the soul

of woman

must be expansive . . .

and open

to all human beings

Section Theme

God has a specific plan for woman. He has given her a holy mission, a holy call.

Section Grace

Pray for the grace of authentic femininity and spiritual motherhood.

Woman: Fearfully and Wonderfully Made

***

"It is not simply an accident of nature that my unique personal selfhood was meant to be clothed, as it were, in a female body. . . . God has chosen from all eternity that I will be a feminine creature. . . . Prayerful pondering of the mystery of creation brings a woman to consider what role God may have chosen for her in his Kingdom, on earth and in heaven."

DR. RONDA CHERVIN

Dear Lord,

From all eternity You chose for me to be a woman. Why? What is it about my femininity that will lead me closer to You? How can my femininity bring Your life to the world? I desire to know more about womanhood and how I can experience the fullness of my feminine call. Teach me Your truth about my gender. Amen.

*B*efore I formed you in the womb I knew you, and before you were born I consecrated you.

— Jeremiah 1:5
(Revised Standard Version)

Daily Reflection

God's actions are deliberate. He chose for me to have life and He gave me life out of love. Are there any potential circumstances of my birth that would seek to convince me otherwise? What are they? How does this revelation of my "selection" by the Father change my perspective?

Everything about me was God's deliberate choice — even my gender. Are there issues I need to resolve about my femininity? Name them. What can I do to overcome them?

Read the last sentence of Dr. Chervin's quote. It suggests that my gift of femininity has a role in the world and in eternity. What might this role be? Consider this in light of my current life and in light of eternity. How does this concept broaden my perspective of my gender?

How do I see my femininity as being "consecrated"? In what ways can my femininity lead me closer to God?

Womanly Ways

"The woman's humanity is realized in the specific ways of a woman. She is a complete human being no less than the man, but according to her *own* nature. Her sex is not a mere accidental condition that could be abstracted. Her sex, on the contrary, is a reality that fundamentally defines her being and acting and corresponds to the specific design of the Creator. Her physical and psychological qualities proclaim clearly what it truly means to be a woman."

JUTTA BURGGRAF

Dear Lord,

My femininity defines my very being. There is so much for me to learn about who You have designed me to be by giving me my female gender. Enlighten my mind to understand what it means to be a woman — in body, mind, and soul. The world has done much to convince me of many things about my sex. Give me clarity to see what is truth and what is not. Amen.

Scripture Passage for Meditation

*I*t was you who created my inmost self, and put me together in my mother's womb; for all these mysteries I thank you: for the wonder of myself, for the wonder of your works. You know me through and through, from having watched my bones take shape when I was being formed in secret, knitted together in the limbo of the womb.

— Psalm 139:13-15
(The Jerusalem Bible)

Daily Reflection

Quietly ponder the great mystery of your conception and birth. Then think of how you have been designed by God as a unique and gifted woman. What about my personhood makes me most grateful to God?

God has created me as an integrated person. What are the connections between physical womanhood, spiritual womanhood, and emotional womanhood?

What does femininity mean to me? What contemporary attitudes about woman conflict with a Christian understanding of who God created her to be? Are there any conflicting attitudes within me? Specifically, what can I do to resolve them according to the light of truth?

What do I see as the role of women today?

The Mystery of Woman

"The profound center of woman's mystery: the whole of created human reality with all its inexhaustible richness, but first of all in its organic unity, is initially present in the microcosm of her body as a shadowy perception which awakens her spirit."

LOUIS BOUYER

Dear Lord,

With the exception of Adam and Eve, every human life that has ever been and every human life that will ever be has been tucked away in the hidden recesses of the female person. What a special gift You have given to woman! How graciously You have chosen her! Help me to appreciate the life-bearing potential of my body. Give me spiritual eyes to see what more this tells me about Your plan for me. Awaken my spirit to the holy and divine call of womanhood. Amen.

Lord, our Lord, how admirable is thy name in the whole earth! For thy magnificence is elevated above the heavens. . . . What is man that thou art mindful of him? Or the son of man that thou visitest him? Thou hast made him a little less than the angels, thou hast crowned him with glory and honor.

— Psalm 8:2, 5-6
(Douay-Rheims)

Daily Reflection

➤ Consider the intricate splendor of the female body in light of its reproductive and nurturing capacity. What strikes you most about the precision with which God has created it? How does this reveal the grandeur of God's divine plan?

❧ Woman participates in a unique way in God's sovereign role of Creator. How does this specially "crown" the female person with God's glory?

❧ Prayerfully ponder the possibility that the feminine ability to bear life may signify a corresponding spiritual reality. What might it be? What other thoughts or insights does this pondering bring?

The Womb of Woman

"In the great act of procreation, the woman . . . gives herself and lets herself be fecundated. The greatness of her role is illustrated by the fact that *she is given but a microscopic seed; she gives back a human being*, made to God's image and likeness. This fact alone should open our eyes to the greatness of . . . the female vocation, for it is in the woman's womb that the fecundated egg receives its soul. The female womb is, therefore, an organ of remarkable dignity."

ALICE VON HILDEBRAND, PH.D.

Dear Lord,

When Your hand places an immortal soul into the babe in the womb, You make the womb a place of sanctity and holiness. But, our culture humiliates this place of honor. It has made the womb a thing of derision, manipulation, and torture. Even woman herself has cooperated in the desecration. Restore to our world a sense of the womb's sanctity, and correct in me any false notion or idea that leads me away from the truth of my femininity. Amen.

Scripture Passage for Meditation

Woe to those who call evil good, and good evil, who put darkness for light, and light for darkness, who put bitter for sweet, and sweet for bitter!
— Isaiah 5:20
(Revised Standard Version)

Daily Reflection

- What are some of the prevailing attitudes in secular society regarding the womb of woman and her reproductive capacity?

- How do the teachings of the Catholic Church contrast with these attitudes? See Appendix, Paragraphs 1652, 2363, 2366, 2367, 2368, and 2370 of the *Catechism of the Catholic Church* (CCC).

🌿 In the quote, Alice Von Hildebrand suggests a supernatural dimension regarding the womb. Ponder this. What deeper understanding does this bring to the sacredness of the womb and the entire reproductive system of woman?

🌿 Contemporary thoughts and ideas often take root in subtle ways. To what extent have my own attitudes about my womb and reproductive system been shaped by the culture of the day? How can I overcome false understandings? Are there specific actions God might be asking me to take personally and in other ways?

The Soul of Woman

"... The soul is the formative principle of the body — *anima corporis forma*. Human nature has two species, male and female. The difference between the bodies of men and women indicates corresponding differences in spirituality and calling."

ANNE ROCHE MUGGERIDGE

Dear Lord,

You have purposed that human persons consist of a body and a soul. Since the soul takes the form of the body, if my body is feminine, then my soul is feminine also. Reveal to me how I can live out the fullness of my gender — in body and soul. May all I do be consistent with who You have chosen me to be — a female person created in Your image and likeness. Amen.

*T*hen God said: "Let us make man in our image, after our likeness. . . ." So God created man in his own image, in the image of God he created him; male and female he created them.

— Genesis 1:26, 27
(Revised Standard Version)

Daily Reflection

🕊 God has created the female person to share in His sovereign act of bringing new life to the world. Her body reflects this. If the soul is the "immediate substantial" form of the body (Council of Vienne, 1311-1312), what does the life-bearing potential of the female body indicate about the soul of woman?

🕊 Could there be a relationship between a contraceptive mentality and a contraceptive spirituality?

The soul of woman must be *expansive* **37**

By purposefully frustrating the conjugal act and preventing herself from exercising her feminine charism to bear life physically, could a woman prevent herself from experiencing the fullness of spiritual life?

🌿 How can my soul be life-giving for myself? For others?

🌿 How can this aspect of my being be nurtured?

The Nature of Woman

"Woman's nature is determined by her original vocation of *spouse and mother*. One depends on the other. The body of woman is fashioned 'to be one flesh' with another and to nurse new human life in itself."

St. Edith Stein

Dear Lord,

You have woven into the very fabric of the womanly heart a longing to be in loving communion with another — a union that is life-giving and life-sustaining. This is so clearly seen in the nuptial embrace and its openness to life. But, even the feminine soul longs for fertile communion — a communion with You that conceives and nurtures spiritual life. Help me to become a fertile field, ready to receive Your seed of grace. Make me pregnant with Your divine life that I may be made holy and become a source of grace for others. Help me achieve my vocation as a woman. Amen.

⮚⮚⮚⮚⮚⮚⮚⮚⮚⮚⮚⮚⮚

*H*ail, full of grace, the Lord is with you! . . . Do not be afraid, Mary, for you have found favor with God. And behold, you will conceive and bear a son, and you shall call his name Jesus. . . . The Holy Spirit will come upon you and the power of the Most High will overshadow you; therefore the child to be born will be called holy, the Son of God.

— Luke 1:28, 30-32, 35
(Revised Standard Version)

Daily Reflection

Contemplating the virginal conception of Jesus in the Blessed Mother, how does the original vocation of spouse and mother apply to all women — religious, single, and women married without children? How do I see the original vocation represented in me?

🌿 What are some specific ways the Lord uses my feminine call as a source of sanctification for myself? For others?

🌿 Consider the longing to be in loving communion with others and the life-giving and life-sustaining dimensions of such a relationship. Do I seek opportunities to enter into life-giving relationships with others? In what ways? What other opportunities for this exist in my everyday life?

Woman's Gift

"The gift of being a woman is the ability to give life. As Christian women we have an even greater privilege — to give supernatural life to others through a personal relationship with Christ in faith."

MARIANNE EVANS MOUNT

Dear Lord,

Now I come to a deeper understanding of the special gift of woman — she has been called to bring life to the world. But, her physical capacity to bear life reflects a deep spiritual reality — woman is meant to bear spiritual life to the world. Help me to enter into this glorious and divine mission of bringing Your life to others. But first, lead me into an intimate relationship with You. Mold me and shape me into Your very image. Amen.

❧❧❧❧❧❧❧❧❧❧❧❧❧❧❧

I am the vine, you are the branches. He who abides in me and I in him, he it is that bears much fruit. . . . I chose you and appointed you that you should go and bear fruit and that your fruit should abide. . . .

— John 15:5, 16
(Revised Standard Version)

Daily Reflection

❧ According to my state in life, how seriously do I take my call to bring life to others? What challenges face me in fulfilling this call?

❧ Life is communicated in many ways. How do my thoughts, words, and deeds communicate life — in my family, in my community, in the workplace, in my parish, in my recreation?

❧ Am I "abiding" daily in Jesus Christ? How? Looking back over my life, what spiritual "fruit" have I brought forth? Has it "abided"? Has it produced additional fruit?

❧ Throughout the Bible we find many examples of holy women. Consider Esther, Ruth, Deborah, Judith, Anna, Mary Magdalene, and the Blessed Virgin. In your journal, draw a chart consisting of five columns and seven rows (similar to the one on the facing page). Label the columns *Woman, Impact, Attribute, Abiding Fruit,* and *Application.*Complete the chart by recording the impact these women had on the lives of others and/or the culture of their day and time, the attribute or virtue they exhibited, and any "abiding" fruit that came as a result of their attribute or virtue. Then consider how their example applies to your life and/or current situation.

WOMAN	IMPACT	ATTRIBUTE	ABIDING FRUIT	APPLICATION
Esther				
Ruth				
Deborah				
Judith				
Anna				
Mary Magdalene				
Blessed Virgin				

Woman's Spiritual Call

"As Christian women we are called to collaborate in the salvation of the world through the vocation of motherhood, whether it is exercised spiritually or physically. A unique privilege of our Blessed Mother's motherhood was her ability to give Christ to the world both physically and spiritually."

MARIANNE EVANS MOUNT

Dear Lord,

In my imagination, I picture the Blessed Virgin Mary as she enters her cousin Elizabeth's house. What joy she brought there that day! Mary carried Jesus to that home and Salvation entered the soul of Elizabeth and the soul of the baby she carried in her womb! In this, I see Mary as physical mother and spiritual mother. Pregnant with the life of Christ, she "birthed" Him in others. This is the role to which You call all women. May I conceive Jesus in my heart and carry Him to the hearts of others. Amen.

And Mary said, "My soul doth magnify the Lord. And my spirit hath rejoiced in God my Savior. Because he hath regarded the humility of his handmaid; for behold from henceforth all generations shall call me blessed. Because he that is mighty, has done great things for me; and holy is his name."

— Luke 1:46-49
(Douay-Rheims)

Daily Reflection

Through my vocation as woman, the Lord has done great things for me and invites me to do great things in His name. Do I believe this? Identify anything that holds me back from believing this. Surrender this to Jesus.

~ To be willing to undertake great things for God and for our neighbor is called magnanimity. It presupposes greatness of soul and nobility of character. How does the Blessed Mother demonstrate this virtue? To what extent is this virtue present in me? Mary's soul magnifies the Lord. What does this mean? To what extent does my soul magnify Him?

~ St. Elizabeth recognized the presence of Jesus in Mary. In what ways is the presence of Jesus evident in me? How do I give "birth" to Him in the everyday circumstances of my life and in the lives of others? Is there more I can do? What?

~ Do I need to make changes (in my thinking, in my activities, in my attitudes) to accommodate my feminine mission? If so, what are they?

Section Two

the soul

of woman must be quiet . . .

so that no weak flame

will be extinguished

by stormy winds

Section Theme

To fulfill your spiritual mission, Jesus must be the center of your life. This can happen through prayer.

Section Grace

Pray for the grace of a holy and intimate prayer time.

The Perfect Woman

"Were we to present . . . the image of the purely developed character of spouse and mother as it should be according to her natural vocation, we must gaze upon the Virgin Mary. In the center of her life stands her son. She awaits His birth in blissful expectation; she watches over His childhood; near or far, indeed wherever He wishes, she follows Him in His ways; she holds the crucified body in her arms; she carries out the will of the departed. But not as her action does she do all this: she is in this the Handmaid of the Lord; she fulfills that to which God has called her."

St. Edith Stein

Dear Lord,

As Mary's Son and Redeemer, You stood in the center of her life. And she gave everything for love of You. Nothing was too great for her — no pain, no joy, no contradiction, not even Calvary. Much holds me back from this open gift of surrender. Perhaps it is because I have not yet placed You in the center of my life. Perhaps it is because I am still too selfish and aware of my own desires. Perhaps it is because my relationship with You needs to be strengthened through prayer. Help me to overcome all that separates me from You. Like Mary, I desire to be a handmaid of the Lord, fulfilling all to which You call me. Amen.

Scripture Passage for Meditation

ut Mary kept all these things, pondering them in her heart.

— Luke 2:19
(Revised Standard Version)

Daily Reflection

Jesus is the center of Mary's life. Is He the center of my life? Answer this question by picturing your life as a circle. Is Jesus in the center? If not, how close is He to the center? Is He in the circle at all? Use the circles below to illustrate where Jesus currently is in your life

and where you would like Him to be. Place and
name what else fills your life's circle and where it
should be.

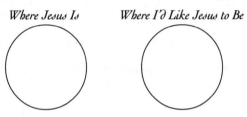

Where Jesus Is   *Where I'd Like Jesus to Be*

❧ What can I do to make Jesus the center of my
life? Which one strategy am I willing to implement now?

❧ What is the benefit of daily prayer? How does
daily prayer help in my relationship with Jesus?
Read Paragraph 2744 (CCC) in the Appendix.

❧ Luke 2:19 says that Mary pondered in her heart
all of her life's circumstances. This is another
way of saying that Mary brought everything in
her life to prayer. To what extent do I ponder my
daily situations in prayer? How can doing so
help me come to a deeper understanding of
God's activity in my life? Do I believe He is "in
all things," even the difficult events of my life?

On Worship and Fulfillment

"The more we give ourselves up in the worship of God, the more our personality is deepened and enriched. The more we concentrate on ourselves and our own status, however, the more we grow poor, shallow, and dull. It is not by accident that today the instances of depression and nervous breakdown are on the rise among women whose sense of identity is confused. We should not forget that only by our living contact with the personal God can we grow beyond our own limitations."

JUTTA BURGGRAF

Dear Lord,

In my journey through life, I have tried many ways to experience fulfillment, and none of them have satisfied. Because You have fashioned me in Your image and likeness, only in You can I find my true self, and only through You can I grow beyond my weaknesses and frailties. Teach me to pray. Teach me to worship You. Lead me along these paths that I might be in communion with You and experience the fullness of life that You intend for me. Amen.

Scripture Passage for Meditation

*Y*et whatever gains I had, these I have come to regard as loss because of Christ. More than that, I regard everything as loss because of the surpassing value of knowing Christ Jesus my Lord. For his sake I have suffered the loss of all things, and I regard them as rubbish, in order that I may gain Christ and be found in him, . . .

— Philippians 3:7-9
(New Revised Standard Version)

Daily Reflection

🐚 What are some of the ways I have sought to find fulfillment and satisfaction on my own? Some means may include social life, possessions, shopping, drugs, alcohol, career, money, and security, even family and friends. Have these means "deepened and enriched my personality" or have they left me wanting? In what ways?

🐚 Worship is defined as "extreme devotion or intense love shown toward God." How do I worship God? Would I describe it as extreme devotion? Intense love? Is my worship confined to Sundays at Mass? How can I worship God in my everyday life?

🐚 Burggraf says that "depression and nervous breakdown are on the rise among women whose sense of identity is confused." How has the contemporary culture "confused" the identity of woman? Is my identity confused? Whose standard do I use to define myself?

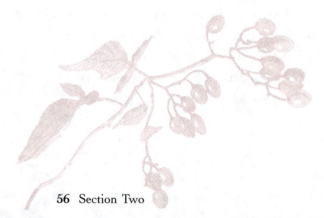 Romans 12:2 says not to conform to this "age" but to be transformed by renewing our minds. What standards can I apply to renew my mind? What are some practical means I can use to renew my mind?

Raising Our Hearts and Minds to God

"Before prayer, endeavor to realize whose Presence you are approaching, and to whom you are about to speak. We can never fully understand how we ought to behave towards God, before whom the angels tremble. . . . I know that many persons who say vocal prayers are raised by God to high contemplation without their knowing how . . . and mental prayer, in my view, is nothing but friendly intercourse and frequent solitary conversations, with him Who we know loves us."

ST. TERESA OF ÁVILA

Dear Lord,
Open my heart to experience a true life of prayer. Guide
me down this path that leads to the springs of living water
and everlasting life. May my prayers be spoken from my
heart. May each word that leaves my lips express my love

and affection. May I experience frequent and wonderful conversations with You. In humility I stand before You, awestruck to be given such a divine invitation. You are my Lord and my God! Amen.

Scripture Passage for Meditation

*B*ut when you go to pray, go to your room and shut the door and pray to your Father who is in secret; and your Father who sees in secret will reward you.

— Matthew 6:6
(Revised Standard Version)

Daily Reflection

Read the excerpt from *Full of Grace: Women and the Abundant Life* in the Appendix. What are my favorite vocal prayers? How can I pray them with greater reverence and devotion?

In what ways do I practice spontaneous vocal prayer? Do these words spring from the abundance of my heart or are they "noisy gongs clanging"? How can ejaculations interspersed throughout the day help to cultivate an ongoing attitude of prayer in me?

How conversational is my prayer with Jesus? Would I consider it to be mental prayer? What can I do to cultivate mental prayer in my prayer time?

Jesus tells me to go to my room, shut the door, and pray in private. How does my prayer environment contribute to my time of prayer? What can I do to make my prayer "closet" a help and not a hindrance to my prayer?

The Words of My Heart

"Even though [Sacred Scriptures] have been fixed in their phrasing for thousands of years, He Who makes us hear them today already had us in mind when He inspired them of old, and he is always present to address Himself to us through them, as if they were at this instant pronounced for the first time."

LOUIS BOUYER

Dear Lord,

What a great gift You have given me through Sacred Scripture! Your words touch my heart. They heal me and give me guidance. They bless me and give me wisdom. They encourage me and give me hope. They assure me and give me confidence. They teach me and nurture me to life. Through Your Word, You are present to me. You speak to me. You transform me. May my thirst for You never cease. May my desire for You ever increase. May Your Word pierce my soul, consume my heart, and form my days. Amen.

Scripture Passage for Meditation

*Y*our word is a lamp for my feet,
a light for my path.

— Psalm 119:105
(Revised Standard Version)

Daily Reflection

- The Vatican II document *Dei Verbum* (Dogmatic Constitution on Divine Revelation) says that in Sacred Scripture, God comes lovingly to meet His children and talk to them. Have I had this experience? Recall it.

- Why should prayerful reading of Scripture be part of my prayer time?

- Do I know how to pray the Scriptures? Following is a series of questions to make a time of Scripture-praying fruitful. Am I willing to try this method (called *Lectio Divina*) for one week to see its effects? If not, why do I resist?

Ask:

1. What does this passage mean?
2. What is happening in it?
3. What is God saying? To whom is He saying it?
4. Given my current circumstance or situation, what is God saying to me personally? What grace is He offering me through these words?
5. What sentiments or emotions does this passage draw from me? What causes me to feel as I do? How do I wish to respond to the generosity of God's grace?

Go back and use this method for the Scripture passage and the quotation for this meditation. Journal your insights. For the rest of the Meditations in *Grace-Filled Moments*, use this method of *Lectio Divina* as you pray the quotations and the Scripture passages.

❧ Think about Louis Bouyer's statement that God "already had us in mind" at the moment He first inspired the Scriptures. What is my reaction? What thoughts, inspirations, and emotions well up within me?

The Bouquet of Prayer

"A few moments of recollection and meditation each morning in the presence of God transforms and perfumes the whole day, like flowers cast about when night comes, whose fragrance at dawn anoints everything they have touched."

ELISABETH LESEUR

Dear Lord,

Just as prayer perfumes my day with Your fragrant presence, so too do I want to be an odor of sanctity in the world. I want to be a woman who carries the sweet fragrance of Your love to everyone she meets. In the quiet of the morning, draw my heart to You. Open my soul with the breath of Your Holy Spirit. Imbue me with the scent of divine life. Let my words and my actions, my thoughts and my deeds, become bouquets of charity that bring healing, hope, and life. Make me a prayer that is recollected in You. Amen.

Scripture Passage for Meditation

Thanks be to God, who in Christ always leads us in triumph, and through us spreads the fragrance of the knowledge of him everywhere. For we are the aroma of Christ to God among those who are being saved and among those who are perishing, to one a fragrance from death to death, to the other a fragrance from life to life.

— 2 Corinthians 2:14-16
(Revised Standard Version)

Daily Reflection

How can prayer perfume the day? How can a meditative reading of Scripture, using the method given in "The Words of My Heart," become a pleasant fragrance for my soul?

How does prayer make *me* a fragrant odor in my daily life? Consider this in light of prayer's effects in relationships, accepting daily trials, dealing with major contradictions and pain, accomplishing the work of the day. Am I an aroma of Christ? How can I strive to be so every day?

Elisabeth Leseur refers to two types of prayer — meditation and recollection. Consult the Appendix for a definition of both. Do I sincerely desire to make progress in the spiritual life? If I do, what steps must I take to follow through on this desire? What aspects of my daily life could be a hindrance? How can I overcome them?

The Vigilant Soul

"We must pray without ceasing, in every occurrence and employment of our lives — that prayer which is rather a habit of lifting up the heart to God as in a constant communion with Him."

ST. ELIZABETH ANN SETON

Dear Lord,

Prayer must be the melody of my heart that imbues every moment of the day. And yet, so many events and situations cry for my attention. In those moments when much crowds around me, let my soul always be united to You even if my mind may be dealing with what is at hand. Provide a space within me, Jesus, where You and You alone reside. Throughout the day, take me to this interior sanctuary to speak to You, to learn from You, to be with You. In these ways, my prayer can be a stream of life flowing within me and from me to the world. Amen.

Scripture Passage for Meditation

*R*ejoice always, pray constantly.
. . . May the God of peace himself
sanctify you wholly; and may your
spirit and soul and body be kept
sound and blameless at the coming
of our Lord Jesus Christ.

— 1 Thessalonians 5:16, 23
(Revised Standard Version)

Daily Reflection

🍂 Prayer is a discipline. It requires faithful attention to discover its riches. How can I discipline
myself to turn my thoughts and attention to God
during the course of the day? What are some
practical strategies?

🍂 To pray constantly sounds impossible. But God
does not call me to a task for which He hasn't
given me the grace. Daily prayer opens the
windows of my soul to behold Him in every-

thing. St. Stanislaus Kostka said, "I find a heaven in the midst of saucepans and brooms." How can I train my spiritual vision to see His hand in all things — even in the midst of daily chores and pressing concerns in the workplace? How, then, can I surrender each activity to Him?

When a soul is in the state of grace (only mortal sin removes sanctifying grace from a soul), God inhabits it. How can this truth help me in my desire to "pray constantly"?

Prayer and Love

"If you have learned how to pray, then I am not afraid for you. If you know how to pray, then you will love prayer — and if you love to pray, then you will pray. Knowledge will lead to love and love will lead to service."

MOTHER TERESA OF CALCUTTA

Dear Lord,

Everything must start with prayer. If I am to grow in holiness, if I am to discover the truth of who I am as a woman, if I am to be a light in the world today, if my actions are to be imbued with Your life, then I must pray. Only if my works are fortified and strengthened through prayer can they merit any good in my life or in the lives of others. Only if my works are filled with the love that flows from Your heart into mine can they heal, soothe, and set free. May each thought, word, and deed that characterizes my life come from the moments I spend with You. Amen.

Blessed be the God and Father of our Lord Jesus Christ, who has blessed us in Christ with every spiritual blessing in the heavenly places, even as he chose us in him before the foundation of the world, that we should be holy and blameless before him. He destined us in love. . . .

— Ephesians 1:3-5
(Revised Standard Version)

Daily Reflection

There is a difference between a humanitarian act and an act of charity. A humanitarian act can only go so far because it comes from natural inclinations. An act of charity, however, carries grace with it, and thus has the power to transform. In light of this, why is prayer so important for the mission to which I have been called?

- Why is prayer a conduit of love? Have I noticed this to be true in my own relationships — what has been the effect of prayer?

- Prayer places us in the crucible of the Father's love. His flames heal us and purify us. To what extent do I accept or resist this grace in prayer?

- What is the effect of healing and purification on our ability to accept God's love and share it with others? What effect do my healing and purification have on my mission of spiritual motherhood?

Section Three

the soul

of woman must be warm . . .

so as not to benumb

fragile buds

❧❦❧❦❧❦❧❦❧❦❧❦❧❦❧❦❧❦

Section Theme

Certain qualities define the authentically feminine personality.

Section Grace

Pray for the grace to identify, cultivate, and acquire the feminine virtues.

Woman: Full of Grace

"... God, in the sublime event of the Incarnation of his Son, entrusted himself to the ministry ... of a woman. It can thus be said that women, by looking to Mary, find in her the secret of living their femininity with dignity and of achieving their own true advancement. In the light of Mary, the Church sees in the face of woman the reflection of a beauty which mirrors the loftiest sentiments of which the human heart is capable: the self-offering totality of love; the strength that is capable of bearing the greatest sorrows; limitless fidelity and tireless devotion to work; the ability to combine penetrating intuition with words of support and encouragement."

POPE JOHN PAUL II

Dear Lord,

You entrusted Mary to bring the life of Jesus Christ into the world and, like her, You ask me to birth Him in the lives of others. This is my ministry as woman. Help me to conceive the Divine Life in the womb of my soul; help me to nurture the Divine Life in the recesses of my heart; help me to sustain the Divine Life through the integrity of my will; help me to reflect the Divine Life through virtues of generosity, fortitude, fidelity, devotion, compassion, and hope. In this lie dignity and joy. This is the secret of my true advancement. This is the secret of warming others with Your love. Amen.

Scripture Passage for Meditation

Mary set out at that time and went as quickly as she could to a town in the hill country of Judah. She went into Zechariah's house and greeted Elizabeth. Now as soon as Elizabeth heard Mary's greeting, the child leaped in her womb and Elizabeth was filled with the Holy Spirit. She gave a loud cry and said, "Of all women you are the most blessed, and blessed is the fruit of your womb. Why should I be honored with a visit from the mother of my Lord? For the moment your greeting reached my ears, the child in my womb leaped for joy. Yes, blessed is she who believed that the promise made her by the Lord would be fulfilled."

— Luke 1:39-45
(The Jerusalem Bible)

Daily Reflection

What role do my soul, my heart, and my will have in helping me conceive the Divine Life within? How does the condition of each affect my relationship with Jesus Christ? Which of these areas of my being need some attention to help me be spiritually fertile?

Pope John Paul II lists several attributes that reflect the presence of Jesus Christ in a woman's life. What are they? Using Scripture to guide me, how do I see these attributes in the Blessed Virgin Mary?

How do the virtues of generosity, fortitude, fidelity, devotion, compassion, and hope "warm the hearts of others"? How do they help others come to an experience of Jesus Christ in their lives? In which of these ways have I been a Christ-bearer? Share and record the incident(s).

Womanly Influence in the World

"What is it that is missing in this modern world of ours, despite all its outward splendor, its technology and economic progress? . . . Nothing defines the condition of our time more profoundly and tragically than the total absence of all motherly dispositions. . . . It is that minimum of kindness, motherliness, mercy, sense of tact and tenderness which comes from woman as her contribution to the life of man."

GERTRUD VON LE FORT

Dear Lord,

So delicate is the balance brought to the world through the complementarity of the sexes! You have endowed each gender with specific qualities and attributes designed to bring stability and order to the world of man. When this balance is disturbed, confusion, injustice, and pain result. Our culture has sought to convince woman that only by eliminating those characteristics essential to her femininity can she attain advancement and prestige. Such a notion puts woman at risk, and the world, too. Help me to live the true call of my femininity. Help me to bring to my world those qualities specific to my gender. Help me to protect and preserve the holy balance that You have created. Let me be the light of Your love. Amen.

Scripture Passage for Meditation

$\mathcal{P}$ut on then as God's chosen ones, holy and beloved, heartfelt compassion, kindness, lowliness, meekness, and patience, forbearing one another and, if one has a complaint against another, forgiving each other; as the Lord has forgiven you, so you also must forgive. And above all these things put on love, which binds everything together in perfect harmony.

— Colossians 3:12-13
(Revised Standard Version)

Daily Reflection

Within my own community (social, spiritual, political), in what specific ways can I see the consequences of the absence of "motherly" dispositions as outlined by Gertrud von le Fort? In the broader context of society, what current social problems could be at least partially attributed to the same?

Given the notion of spiritual motherhood, how do I define "motherliness"? How do kindness, mercy, tact, and tenderness bring spiritual, emotional, and psychological life?

How can I better live these attributes of the feminine reality within the context of my own circumstances — family, vocation, professional life, parish? Which virtues listed in the passage from Colossians have I acquired? Which do I most need to attain?

Nurturing Life

"That women have been given a special understanding for the deep link existing between suffering and love cannot be contested, because it is linked to their maternal vocation. Not all women have fruits of their own womb, but all women are called upon to be mothers: that is, self-giving, self-sacrificing in the silence of their loving heart."

ALICE VON HILDEBRAND, PH.D.

Dear Lord,

The supreme mission of my life is to be "mother." This mission does not depend upon the fertility of my womb, nor does it depend upon my state in life. Rather, it issues forth from You and who You created me to be as woman. However, my mission does require a response from me. It requires the surrender of my will, the receptivity of my soul, and the fertility of my heart. Teach me, Lord, to be self-giving. Teach me to be self-sacrificing. Teach me to be self-effacing. Let me love with the fullness of my being and help me to love others into life. Amen.

Scripture Passage for Meditation

*T*ruly, truly, I say to you, unless a grain of wheat falls into the earth and dies, it remains alone; but if it dies, it bears much fruit.

— John 12:24
(Revised Standard Version)

Daily Reflection

⌘ Alice Von Hildebrand makes a connection between suffering and love. How and why are they intrinsic to the maternal vocation? How does John 12:24 clarify the relationship between suffering and love?

⌘ How have other women nurtured me in my life through love and sacrifice? Consider all manner of nurturing (spiritual, emotional, physical, psychological). Be specific.

🐦 In what ways can I nurture life in others? Am I willing to make the sacrifice?

🐦 Sometimes we do not receive the nurturing we need. Such a loss can cause emotional, spiritual, or psychological suffering. God wants to bring us to wholeness. Ask these questions and answer honestly:

1. Was I inadequately nurtured at any time in my life? When and how?
2. What emotions did I feel at the time or as I reflect upon it now?
3. Can I name specific ways this has affected me even to the present day?

Each day invite God into this area of suffering and cooperate with the grace He gives to move forward in the healing process.

Loving Those in Our Midst

"It is easy to love the people far away. It is not always easy to love those close to us. It is easier to give a cup of rice to relieve hunger than to relieve the loneliness and pain of someone unloved in our own home. Bring love into your home, for this is where our love for each other must start."

MOTHER TERESA OF CALCUTTA

Dear Lord,

How true are these words written by Mother Teresa! Though I am ashamed to admit it, sometimes I have patience for everyone but my family members. The daily irritations seem to mount until they become almost insurmountable. At times, my lack of charity stems from fatigue, or my physical condition, or mental strain, or the stress of just living. Help me to overcome these obstacles to love. Give me the grace I need to be You to all whom You entrust to me. Amen.

new commandment I give to you, that you love one another; even as I have loved you, that you also love one another. By this all men will know that you are my disciples, if you have love for one another.

— John 13:34
(Revised Standard Version)

Daily Reflection

See the Appendix for a listing of the corporal and spiritual works of mercy. Mother Teresa's statement implies that corporal works of mercy are often easier to perform than spiritual works of mercy? Why?

Is there a family member or community member who currently is difficult to love? What is causing the difficulty? How can I bring love into this situation? Which work of mercy does it require? Which feminine quality?

🌿 What trait(s) do I see in this person that I can thank God for? Begin to thank Him for this trait or virtue. How does this trait help me to see God in this person? How can this realization encourage me to express love to him/her in spite of the current difficulty?

🌿 Is it possible that fatigue, overwork, stress, or my own physical condition could be limiting my ability to exercise charity? If so, in what specific and practical ways can I take better care of myself physically, spiritually, and emotionally? What one way can I begin to implement today?

Life-Giving Words

"The virtuous woman respects the tastes, inclinations, and opinions of others in all that is not contrary to conscience. With ingenious tact, she draws attention to her neighbor's virtues, speaks about edifying things she has seen, and wields more influence by such delicacy than she would by calling attention to faults. Always amiable and patient, she endures all kinds of disappointments and frustrations with a serene countenance, without anger or resentment."

FATHER JAMES ALBERIONE, S.S.P., S.T.D.

Dear Lord,

The spoken word is powerful! In fact, You created the world through the spoken word (see Genesis 1). Because I am made in Your image and likeness, my words create as well. They can create an environment that is life-giving, or they can create an environment that is life-threatening. Show me how to use my tongue to create unity rather than disharmony, to bring resolution rather than dissension, to yield love rather than bitterness, to build up rather than to tear down, to give life rather than to bring death. Amen.

Scripture Passage for Meditation

For out of the abundance of the heart the mouth speaks. The good man out of his good treasure brings forth good, and the evil man out of his evil treasure brings forth evil. I tell you, on the day of judgment men will render account for every careless word they utter; . . .

— Matthew 12:34-36
(Revised Standard Version)

Daily Reflection

What do my words tell me about the abundance of my heart? For the next week, do a daily examination of conscience on the issue of words.

Are my words life-giving or life-threatening? How does this affect my mission of spiritual motherhood?

To what extent do I respect the tastes, inclinations, and opinions of others? How do my actions and words show this? Do I draw attention to my neighbor's strengths or his/her weaknesses? Would someone consider me to be a gossip?

Refer to the Appendix and read about *detraction, calumny, slander,* and *rash judgment.* How are these antithetical to true femininity and the mission of spiritual motherhood? Have I been the source of any of these? Have I been the recipient? Were there long-term effects? What were they? Do they still exist?

St. Angela Merici says, "You will effect more by kind words and a courteous manner, than by anger or sharp rebukes. . . ." How have I seen this to be true in my relationships? Do I exercise patience and tact in the face of confrontation? What strategies can I employ to do so?

Self-Giving Love

"One should always remember that such virtues as surrender, humility, obedience, and the ability to serve and sacrifice presuppose a high degree of spiritual activity, enabling one to ignore one's own selfish demands. Mary is never servile but free and responsible."

JUTTA BURGGRAF

Dear Lord,

Help me to step outside myself and see my actions objectively. Have I surrendered completely to You? Am I obedient? Do I sacrifice for others and serve them in love? Does humility mark my actions? My desire is to grow in virtue and grace and to live my call to spiritual motherhood with true compassion and concern for others. Put to death within me all self-seeking, all pride, all disordered motivation, and help me to serve You with purity of heart. Amen.

*D*o nothing from selfishness or conceit, but in humility count others better than yourselves. Let each of you look not only to his own interests, but to the interests of others.

— Philippians 2:3-4
(Revised Standard Version)

Daily Reflection

❧ Archbishop Fulton J. Sheen said that "pride disguises itself under the prettier names of *success* and *popularity*." To what extent are these motivating forces in my life?

❧ Think through Jutta Burggraf's statement that Mary is never servile but free and responsible. What is the difference between a servile action and a free and responsible one? Which marks my service to others? My relationship with God?

Humility has many counterfeits. Among them are denying our gifts and talents, feigned disregard for compliments or praise, a fear to attempt great things, complacency toward the spiritual life. To what extent do these match with my concept of humility?

One great saint says that true humility is simply "walking in the truth." This means walking in the truth of who we are and Who God is and recognizing that everything of worth comes from Him. How does this definition match the Gospel accounts of the Blessed Virgin?

St. Teresa of Ávila says, "Unless you strive after virtues and practice them, you will never grow to be more than dwarfs." Do I strive after humility? The following four ways will help me grow in humility:

1. Contemplating the majesty of God.
2. Contemplating the person of Jesus Christ.
3. Developing an active prayer life that includes at least fifteen minutes per day of mental prayer.

4. Accepting the contradictions of daily life as opportunities to grow in holiness.

Am I willing to invest myself in them? And, how can I follow through?

 In what specific ways will true humility contribute to my mission of spiritual maternity and warm the hearts of others?

A Consoling Angel

"The Christian woman is the consoling angel of the family. She is a perfume which diffuses itself throughout the house, an oil which reduces or eliminates entirely the friction produced by personality clashes or serious character defects."

FATHER JAMES ALBERIONE, S.S.P., S.T.D.

Dear Lord,

To be a "consoling angel" is to soothe, to comfort, to heal. For me to spiritually mother in this way I need wisdom, insight, and empathy. Fill me with these attributes that I might be a perfume of your love in my family, my community, my workplace, my parish. Help me to share in the burdens of others, to enter into their woundedness and pain. Help me to be an agent of peace between disputing parties, and to offer sound advice and spiritual guidance to those who need it. I want to diffuse the fragrance of your love everywhere. Amen.

Scripture Passage for Meditation

*B*ut the fruit of the Spirit is love, joy, peace, patience, kindness, goodness, faithfulness, gentleness, self-control.

— Galatians 5:22
(Revised Standard Version)

Daily Reflection

❧ Am I a "consoling angel" within the community of the family, the workplace, or my parish? What personal characteristics make me so? Which do not?

❧ What is the difference between a "consoling angel" and a busybody? Consider the motivations and intentions of each. From which of these do my actions flow?

How do the fruit of the Holy Spirit, outlined in the Scripture passage, help me to be a "consoling angel"?

What personality clashes presently exist in my sphere(s) of influence? Is God asking me to be a "consoling angel" in this (these) situation(s)? What makes me think so or think not? What are some practical steps I can take to help eliminate the friction?

Section Four

the soul
of woman must be clear . . .
so that no vermin
will settle in dark corners
and recesses

Section Theme

Self-knowledge and a genuine examination of conscience are essential for authentic femininity and its mission.

Section Grace

Pray for the grace of self-knowledge and true repentance for sin.

Crystal Clear

"Our souls should be like a transparent crystal through which God can be perceived. Our crystal is sometimes covered with dirt and dust. . . . God will help us to remove that dust, as long as we allow him to; if that is our will, His will comes about."

MOTHER TERESA OF CALCUTTA

Dear Lord,

Is my soul like a transparent crystal through which You can be perceived? I fear not. My soul is clouded with the stain of sin, the fog of self-will, the haze of worldly attachments. I desire to be a mirror of Your life within me — to magnify You as did Mary, the Blessed Virgin. Mother Teresa of Calcutta says that You will remove the soot of our souls if we allow You. I will it! May Your will come about in me. Amen.

*I*n a great house there are not only vessels of gold and silver but also of wood and earthenware, and some for noble use, some for ignoble. If any one purifies himself from what is ignoble, then he will be a vessel for the master of the house, ready for any good work. So shun youthful passions and aim at righteousness, faith, love, and peace, along with those who call upon the Lord from a pure heart.

— 2 Timothy 2:20-22
(Revised Standard Version)

Daily Reflection

Sometimes our soul is covered with "dirt and dust" and we are not aware of it. A poorly formed conscience can make us blind to the reality of our spiritual condition. Consult the Appendix for a definition of "conscience" and what it is supposed to do. What has formed my conscience? (Consider Scripture, the Ten Commandments, the Beatitudes, the culture of the day.)

- Do I make a conscious effort to evaluate my actions, my proposed actions, or actions that I have already performed in light of my conscience? Why or why not?

- To what extent do I strive to integrate *every area of my life* with my commitment of faith? Are there some areas of my life that I don't want to hold up to that standard? What are they? Why do I resist?

- According to the guidelines established by the Scripture passage, what kind of vessel am I? To what extent do I conform to the directive given in the last sentence?

- What is the relationship between a well-formed conscience and spiritual motherhood?

Self-Knowledge: A Necessity for Holiness

"Much as we want to know ourselves, we do not really know ourselves. Do we really want to see ourselves as God sees us, or even as our fellow human beings see us? Could we bear it, weak as we are? . . . We do not want to be given that clear inward vision which discloses to us our most secret faults. In the Psalms there is that prayer, 'Deliver me from my secret sins.' We do not really know how much pride and self-love we have . . . we are ashamed."

DOROTHY DAY

Dear Lord,

I say that I want to see myself as You see me, and then I cower at the thought of what I might discover. I am weak; fill me with courage. I am blind; give me inward vision. I deceive myself; teach me truth. I am a sinner; show me your mercy. I am prideful; humble me with self-knowledge.

Deliver me from my "secret sins" and set me free through knowledge of the truth. Amen.

⟨⟩or the grace of God has appeared for the salvation of all men, training us to renounce irreligion and worldly passions, and to live sober, upright, and godly lives in this world, awaiting our blessed hope, the appearing of the glory of our great God and Savior, Jesus Christ, . . .

— Titus 2:11-13
(Revised Standard Version)

Daily Reflection

Consult the Appendix and read the entry under "Conscience Formation." How does the conscience become properly formed? What can I do to "train" my conscience? Am I willing to make the effort? Why or why not?

- In the Appendix, read the entry "Erroneous Conscience." Using the definitions, could my conscience be "erroneously formed"? In what way? Specifically, how has the culture of the day contributed to erroneously formed consciences? Has the contemporary culture influenced my conscience? How?

- Rationalization and habitual sin "deaden" our conscience. Do I have any habitual sin, or have I rationalized any attitude or activity? What is it? Do I believe God will give me the grace to break with it? Do I believe my salvation depends on breaking with it? What can I do to cooperate with God's grace to break with it?

- Am I willing to observe *all* Church teachings? Why or why not? How does this affect my conscience and the condition of my soul?

Know Thyself: The Examination of Conscience

"The first lesson of the heart of Jesus is our examination of conscience: know thyself. The examination of conscience consists of facing ourselves with Jesus. We should not waste time looking at our misery, but we are rather to look into His light."

MOTHER TERESA OF CALCUTTA

Dear Lord,

It is not easy for me to look at the truth about myself. The reality of my condition could cause me to lose hope, except that I know You are beside me, desiring to draw me to Yourself. Send me the light of Your Holy Spirit. Illuminate my areas of weakness. Help me to repent and be set free from all that holds me captive. Give me a willing spirit to break with sin, to avoid rationalization, and to abide by the teachings of Scripture and Holy Mother Church. Amen.

If you continue in my word, you are truly my disciples, and you will know the truth, and the truth will make you free.

— John 8:31-32
(Revised Standard Version)

Daily Reflection

❧ When was the last time I made a sincere examination of conscience? What benefits would I receive by doing so on a daily basis? To make a daily examination requires some discipline and some effort. Is my spiritual life worth it?

❧ Consult the Appendix and read the section entitled "How to Make an Examination of Conscience." List the four steps Father Tanquerey recommends for making the examination of conscience. In what way does a daily examination help to heal our spiritual blindness?

Could I be spiritually blind in any way? To what?

~ Mother Teresa says that we are to face our examination with Jesus and focus our attention on His light. Father Tanquerey says that we are to picture Jesus before us as the "Divine Model" and as the "Healer of Souls." In what ways can these images of Jesus help me to make a good examination? How can seeing Jesus as healer begin to set me free?

~ Consider Jesus as the "Healer of Souls." Which area of my soul would He most want to heal? How could a healing in this area positively impact on my mission of spiritual motherhood?

Know Thyself: The Particular Examine

"When you are tormented by any passion or evil inclination, if you be so weak as to yield to it, and let it lead you, take it for a certain truth, that it will take deeper root, wage a more violent war against you. But if you resist it courageously at first, it will daily diminish. Every day it will have less strength to act upon you, till at length, it will come to have none at all."

ST. DOROTHEUS

Dear Lord,

Certain weaknesses, frailties, and sins have become lifelong habits. These are very hard to break. And yet, I desire to put them far from me because they lead me away from You. Reveal to me that one sin which has the greatest hold on me. Help me to cooperate with the grace You are giving me to overcome it. May I make progress in the path to holiness and be a light that leads others to You. Amen.

So put away all malice and all guile and insincerity and envy and all slander. Like newborn babes, long for the pure spiritual milk, that by it you may grow up to salvation; for you have tasted the kindness of the Lord.

— 1 Peter 2:1-3
(Revised Standard Version)

Daily Reflection

How can sinful inclinations take deeper root in us according to St. Dorotheus? What is the remedy? Refer to the Appendix. What is a "particular examine (or examination)" of conscience? How does it comply with the Scripture passage? What weakness, frailty, or sinful inclination is my predominant fault? What are its outward manifestations? Am I willing to wage a holy war against it through a particular examination? Why or why not?

- ❧ St. John Vianney said, "The devil only tempts those souls that wish to abandon sin and those that are in a state of grace. The others belong to him; he has no need to tempt them." Based on this quote, what can I expect as I enter into the habit of a particular examination? To what extent will this "advanced warning" help me in my quest?

- ❧ Consider some of the feminine qualities discussed in Section Three. How can the particular examination help me to acquire them? To what extent can a particular examination help me in my mission of spiritual motherhood? How does this help mark the progress of my spiritual journey?

The Gravity of Sin

"Let us say that the Divinity is like a very clear diamond, much larger than the whole world, or a mirror. . . . Then let us suppose that all we do is seen in this diamond, which is so formed as to contain everything within itself, for there is nothing that can lie outside its greatness. It was a terrifying thing for me to see . . . such ugly things as my own sins reflected in that clearness and purity. . . . If only someone could explain this to those who commit the most ugly and dishonorable sins, they might realize that such deeds are not hidden; that as they are committed in His Majesty's presence, He is justly grieved by them. . . . I saw the way in which hell is actually earned by a single mortal sin, and the impossibility of understanding what a very grave thing it is to commit such a sin before so exalted a Majesty, and I saw how alien to His nature such deeds are."

ST. TERESA OF ÁVILA

Dear Lord,

It is hard for me to comprehend the gravity of sin and its consequences. How utterly offensive it must be to You Who are Pure Goodness and Pure Holiness. But it offends You still more because sin separates us from You. Today, many people live as if You did not exist. I must admit that sometimes my own thoughts, words, and deeds would suggest as much. How this must hurt You Who are Pure Love. Give me the interior strength to resist all sin and to live in the light of Your love. Amen.

Scripture Passage for Meditation

If we say we have no sin, we deceive ourselves, and the truth is not in us. If we confess our sins, he is faithful and just, and will forgive our sins and cleanse us from all unrighteousness.

— 1 John 1:8-9
(Revised Standard Version)

The soul of woman must be *clear* **113**

Daily Reflection

❧ "Sin is an offense against reason, truth, and right conscience" and "an offense against God" (CCC, § 1849, § 1850). Moral theology divides the gravity of sin into two categories — mortal and venial. Consult the Appendix. What constitutes a mortal sin? What are the three conditions for mortal sin? Based on this information, am I in mortal sin? Is it a recurring sin in my life? What is the remedy?

❧ Some believe that the only "dangerous" sin is mortal sin. However, St. Thérèse of Lisieux says, "You ought to make every effort to free yourselves even from venial sin, and to do what is most perfect." Refer to the Appendix. What is venial sin? What are its effects? What venial sins do I most commonly commit? What are some practical ways I can overcome these sins?

❧ The prevailing moral condition of our time is a loss of the sense of sin. How have the following factors contributed to the decline: cultural and ethical relativism, incorrect statements of popular psychology, the confusion between morality and legality, secularism/humanism? To what extent have any of these affected me? Does my conduct reflect Christian truth in all areas of my life?

"A Communion of Sin"

"One can speak of 'a communion of sin,' whereby a soul that debases itself through sin drags down with itself the Church and, in some way, the whole world. In other words, there is not a single sin, not even the most intimate and secret one, the most strictly personal and individual one, that exclusively concerns the person committing it. With greater or lesser violence, with consequences of greater or lesser harm, every sin has repercussions on the entire ecclesial body and the whole human family. According to this first meaning of the term, every sin can undoubtedly be considered as *social* sin. . . ."

POPE JOHN PAUL II

Dear Lord,
Sin tears at the moral fabric — whether that sin is public
or private, exterior or interior — because every deed that
we perform, every thought that we think, influences the
world of man to a greater or lesser degree. When I consider

this reality, I shudder at the sins I have committed. To what extent have these sins torn at the delicate fiber of the moral conscience? To what extent have these sins led to other sins — in my life and in the lives of others? Forgive me for the damage I have done. May redemptive grace flow from Your heart into mine, and from my heart to the world. Amen.

Scripture Passage for Meditation

As it is, God has put all the separate parts into the body he chose. . . . If one part is hurt, all the parts share its pain. . . . Now Christ's body is yourselves, each of you with a part to play in the whole.

— 1 Corinthians 12:20, 26, 27
(The New Jerusalem Bible)

Daily Reflection

🍂 In my own life experience, how have I seen sins considered "personal" or "private" negatively affect the lives of others? And then, still others? Have any of these sins been my own?

🍂 Proverbs says, "Uprightness makes a nation great, by sin whole races are disgraced" (Proverbs 14:34). How does this relate to the Scripture passage? In our current culture, how has this proverb held true? What "structures of sin" do we see in our society? What "upright structures" do we see?

🍂 Elisabeth Leseur said, "Every soul that rises above itself, raises up the world." To the law of descent caused by social sin is this corresponding law of ascent. How can the practice of virtue by God's people begin to restore the temporal order? How can my personal practice of virtue help to heal the breach in my own social sphere — family, community, parish, workplace? How is this in keeping with my call to spiritual motherhood?

Confession: The Sacrament of Mercy and Healing

"Confession heals, confession justifies, confession grants pardon of sin. All hope consists in confession. In confession there is a chance for mercy. Believe it firmly. Do not doubt, do not hesitate, never despair of the mercy of God. Hope and have confidence in confession."

ST. ISIDORE OF SEVILLE

Dear Lord,

How gracious is Your mercy! How generous is Your forgiveness! How healing is Your love! You desire that no stain of sin should separate me from You, so in Your abundant love You offer me reconciliation and healing. You offer me new life. You offer me the regenerative waters of forgiveness. Lead me to this sacrament often. Help me to enter this wellspring of Your love with sincerity and humility. Give me knowledge of my sins and true contrition for them. Instill in me a firm purpose of amendment and the honesty to admit my offenses to Your priest. Help me to make my penance with integrity, always aware of Your generous and never-failing love. Restore me. Renew me. Redeem me. May this font of healing fortify and strengthen me for my mission of spiritual motherhood. Amen.

Scripture Passage for Meditation

Have mercy on me, O God, in your faithful love, in your great tenderness wipe away my offences; wash me clean from my guilt, purify me from my sin. . . . God, create in me a clean heart, renew within me a resolute spirit, do not thrust me away from your presence, do not take away from me your spirit of holiness. Give me back the joy of your salvation, sustain in me a generous spirit.

— Psalm 51:1-2, 10-11
(The New Jerusalem Bible)

Daily Reflection

🌿 The prayer gives the five requirements for a good confession. What are they?

🌿 How have I experienced God's mercy in my life? To what extent have I experienced it through the Sacrament of Penance? Recall the moment.

🌿 Some people cite a variety of reasons for staying away from confession: they can go straight to God; they don't commit any serious sins; the priest offended them once; they are afraid. Do any of these apply to me? How can I correct my thinking?

🌿 In *Mystici Corporis Christi*, Pope Pius XII listed the many benefits to frequent confession. Read the quotation in the Appendix. Which of these benefits have I experienced?

🍂 Consider the following and journal your thoughts:
1. The effect of sin on personality.
2. The effect of sin on wholeness and health.
3. The effect of sin on our gifts and talents.
4. The overall effect of the denial of sin.

🍂 St. Isidore says that confession is healing. How have I experienced the healing power of the Sacrament of Penance (emotional, psychological, spiritual, physical)?

🍂 Name some ways in which the Sacrament of Penance can impact on my mission of spiritual motherhood.

Section Five

the soul

of woman must be

self-contained . . .

so that no invasions

from without

can peril the inner life

Section Theme

Perils of the interior life present a threat to our relationship with God and our mission of spiritual motherhood.

Section Grace

Pray for the grace to identify and resist all threats to the life of God within you.

The Peril of Lukewarmness

"Pay the greatest attention to this: that your heart be ever glowing with love. Boiling water does not attract flies, lukewarm water does. In the same way the devil with all his impure thoughts shuns and keeps his distance from the soul aglow with love for God. To the tepid soul and the one growing cold in his love for God the flies of vanity and useless thoughts come in swarms. Such souls are submerged and this becomes the source of their baleful negligence and torpor."

BLESSED BAPTISTA VARANO

Dear Lord,

What is the temperature of my soul? Is it burning with love of You? Is it lukewarm? Could it be cold? Stir up the graces of my Baptism until they become a mighty blaze in me. Stoke the fire of my heart with Your holy presence. Let Your eucharistic life glow in me. Ignite all that I think, say, and do with the flame of Your love. Protect me from spiritual sloth and indifference so that I may radiate Your goodness to the world and be a light of Your love to Your people. Amen.

Scripture Passage for Meditation

. . . We want every one of you to show to the very end the same earnestness for the fulfillment of your hopes; so that you may become not sluggish but imitators of those who by faith and patience will inherit the promises.

— Hebrews 6:11-12
(Challoner-Rheims)

Daily Reflection

Father Adolphe Tanquerey in his spiritual classic, *The Spiritual Life,* says that lukewarmness has two causes: "defective spiritual nourishment and the entry into the soul of some noxious germ." He offers the following remedies: *frequent recourse to a wise confessor, fervent practice of the exercises of piety, practice of the virtues*, and *fulfillment of one's duties of state.* Do I suffer from "defective spiritual nourishment" or a "noxious spiritual germ"? What remedies do I most need to implement to either heal or prevent a spiritual malady?

🍂 Great spiritual masters talk about taking "custody" of our senses. By this they mean protecting our souls from any temptation to sin that could enter through the senses. Could any of the following be temptations or occasions of sin for me and should I, therefore, take "custody" of my senses in their regard: movies, television, magazines, shopping, conversations, jokes, music, food, drink, certain relationships? How does avoidance of them help protect my soul?

🍂 One definition for spiritual sloth is "the aversion to one's own moral or spiritual good because of the difficulties in its pursuit" (*Our Sunday Visitor's*

Encyclopedia of Catholic Doctrine, entry by Patrick Lee, 1997, p. 75). Do I find the spiritual life sometimes too difficult to pursue? In what ways? During any specific times or in specific situations? How can a spiritual companion, spiritual friend, or faithful community help me?

Refer to the Appendix and read the entry "A Ladder to Hatred of God." Lukewarmness is but one rung on the ladder. Do any of these apply to me? Which? In what ways? What is the antidote?

The Peril of Worldly Attachments

"In this world we must not become attached to anything — not even things the most innocent, for they fail us at the moment when we are least expecting it. The eternal alone can satisfy us."

ST. THÉRÈSE OF LISIEUX

Dear Lord,

I am a product of my day and culture. Consumerism, sensate pleasures, and vain excitements mark the tenor of our times, and they clamor for my attention, too. Protect me from the attraction of exhaustible riches and preserve me, instead, for the everlasting treasures of eternal life. Give me fortitude to combat temptations, perseverance to renounce passions, and courage to overcome attachments. May my soul be an empty vessel ready to be filled with You and all whom You send to me. Amen.

Do not lay up for yourselves treasures on earth, where moth and rust consume and where thieves break in and steal, but lay up for yourselves treasures in heaven, where neither moth nor rust consumes and where thieves do not break in and steal. For where your treasure is, there will your heart be also.

— Matthew 6:19-21
(Revised Standard Version)

Daily Reflection

Our society is marked by a consumerist mentality. How has this mentality affected me? Consider my use of money and possessions, my view of sensate wants and desires, and how I spend my free time.

❧ St. Thérèse says we "must not become attached to anything. . . ." To fulfill this mandate, we must acquire a spirit of detachment. Refer to the Appendix and answer the questions thoughtfully and prayerfully. What conclusions have I come to? What resolutions?

❧ St. Francis de Sales tells us that we may possess riches without being poisoned by them provided we have them for use and not by love in our heart. Are my possessions tools that help me live my call, or are they "trophies" that appeal to my pride and sense of accomplishment? How does my answer compare with Matthew 6:19-21? What is the treasure of my heart?

❧ How can attachment to things of the world conflict with my mission of spiritual motherhood?

The Peril of Self-Indulgence

"Far from being like to those great souls who from their childhood practice all sorts of macerations, I made my mortification consist solely in the breaking of my will, restraining a hasty word, rendering little services to those around me without making anything of it, and a thousand other things of this kind."

St. Thérèse of Lisieux

Dear Lord,

How dreadfully self-indulgent I am! I seek what is easy and comfortable and hide from what is difficult and loathsome. I rush to what gives me pleasure and withdraw from that which is unpleasant. I am attracted to that which makes me feel good, but am repelled by that which calls me to accountability. How can I achieve my mission of spiritual motherhood if my heart is rooted in self? Give me perseverance to overcome my selfishness; give me courage to break my will; give me steadfastness to grow in grace. Amen.

Put off your old nature which belongs to your former manner of life and is corrupt through deceitful lusts, and be renewed in the spirit of your minds, and put on the new nature, created after the likeness of God in true righteousness and holiness.

— Ephesians 4:22-23
(Revised Standard Version)

Daily Reflection

❧ What are my areas of self-indulgence? Consider your use of time, talent, treasure, what you talk about a lot, your common excuses.

❧ The antidote to self-indulgence is self-sacrifice or mortification. Mortification consists of bringing our senses and our basic human instincts under subjection to our will in conformity to the will of

God. Specifically, how do I practice generosity of spirit through mortification in my everyday circumstances? How have I demonstrated it today? Yesterday? Consider the ways St. Thérèse mentions. What can I add to these? How can this aid my mission of spiritual motherhood?

The Scripture passage tells us to "put on the new nature." This calls us to train the will. Refer to the Appendix. To what extent is my will supple enough to conform to God and strong enough to control my passions and appetites? Which of the obstacles described (interior and exterior) are most likely to afflict me? Have I been weak in these areas in the past? What can I do to overcome these obstacles? What are the positive means to train the will? How can they help me with the obstacles I have? How can a particular examination of conscience help me?

The Peril of Interior Wounds

"Never must our wounded sensibilities make us indifferent or hardhearted. The wounds that bleed are still alive; let us rejoice if an unconscious hand by touching our wound proves that the tissues are full of life and will one day have a sweet healing through a continual interior action."

ELISABETH LESEUR

Dear Lord,

In so many ways my heart has been wounded, trampled upon, and bruised. You want to expand my soul by filling it with Your love, and yet these wounds render it a leaky vessel, out of which Your love drains. Heal me of the aches of the past and the pains of the present. Reveal in the light of day what has been hidden in the darkness that I might experience the fullness of Your mercy and kindness. Then, touched by Your healing love, let my own suffering become a consolation in the lives of others that they might be set free from misery and hurt. Amen.

Scripture Passage for Meditation

*L*et us exult, too, in our hardships, understanding that hardship develops perseverance, and perseverance develops a tested character, something that gives us hope, and a hope which will not let us down, because the love of God has been poured into our hearts by the Holy Spirit which has been given to us.

— Romans 5:3-5
(The New Jerusalem Bible)

Daily Reflection

🍂 What areas of my personality and character need to experience the healing love of Jesus Christ?

🍂 Can I name the prevailing wound of my heart? What about this memory is most painful? Formulate a prayer inviting Jesus into this difficult moment. Pray it daily for one week. Record any comfort or healing you may experience, insight, or understanding.

🍂 Sometimes it is difficult to discover if we have a wound of the heart. Elisabeth Leseur gives us an example of a good symptom — when a seemingly benign incident, comment, or interaction provokes a painful or disproportionate reaction in us. Has this happened to me? When? Can I remember feeling this way before? Is there anything reminiscent about the situation? How does this cast the light of truth on the situation?

🍂 Elisabeth Leseur says that discovering the wound will bring a "sweet healing through a continual interior action." This suggests that inner healing is a process. To what extent have I experienced this? Am I willing to engage the process? Why or why not?

Why do untended wounds of the heart make us indifferent and hardhearted toward others? Toward God and the things of God? How does this negatively impact on my mission of spiritual motherhood? How can my wounds become a source of consolation for others?

The Peril of an Unforgiving Heart

"To know how to forgive is the special mark of the Christian. Forgiveness should not merely be passive; it should be a lively act of love."

ELISABETH LESEUR

Dear Lord,

Lack of forgiveness chains my heart and binds my spirit. It prevents me from experiencing Your abundant love and it prevents me from being a source of Your love to others. Free me from my captivity. Heal those places where I have been sinned against, those places where injury has been carved into the delicate fiber of my being, those places darkened by the shroud of resentment and bitterness. Give me the desire to forgive. Fill me with Your mercy and help me extend it to the one who hurt me. Amen.

*B*e merciful, even as your Father is merciful. Judge not and you will not be judged; condemn not, and you will not be condemned; forgive, and you will be forgiven; give, and it will be given to you; good measure, pressed down, shaken together, running over, will be put into your lap. For the measure you give will be the measure you get back.

— Luke 6:36-38
(Revised Standard Version)

Daily Reflection

Why and in what way is forgiveness "the special mark of the Christian"? Is there anyone I need to forgive? What was the injury committed against me? Am I willing to enter into the process of forgiveness? Why or why not?

❧ Sometimes forgiveness is difficult because we have a false perception of what it is. Forgiveness is a free-will action prompted by grace that sets us free from the consequence of sin. How does unforgiveness bind us to the sin committed against us? How does it bind the offending party to us? How does forgiveness, then, "set us free from the consequence of sin"?

❧ Forgiveness does not mean I condone the hurtful behavior, that my pain doesn't matter, that everything is okay, that I should allow ill will toward me to continue, that I should stay in an abusive situation, that I should feel forgiveness. How does this clarification encourage me to move forward in the process of forgiveness?

❧ What does the Scripture passage indicate about the relationship between forgiving and being forgiven? Meditate on the following Scripture passages — Matthew 18:21-22, Matthew 5:23-24, Matthew 5:43-48, Matthew 7:2-5, Matthew 6:14, and Ephesians 4:26-27. Write down any personal reflections or lessons gained from these passages.

🌿 How does an unforgiving heart breed bitterness and resentment? How do these affect my relationship with God? With others? In what ways do these emotions constrict my heart? How does this impact on my ability to be a spiritual mother?

The Peril of Discouragement

"In barren times, when duty seems difficult and the daily task has no charm, when all spiritual consolation is refused us, and the beautiful light that gilds life is veiled, then humble prayer alone can uphold us and give us hour by hour and day by day the will to act 'against our will.' "

ELISABETH LESEUR

Dear Lord,

When the pressures of life seem overwhelming, when my daily duties yield little fruit, when I have worked hard at relationships to no avail, I grow discouraged. I lose heart. Fortitude wanes. I become disheartened. In these moments when I am rocked by the waves of life, steady me. Draw me close to Your Sacred Heart. Anchor me in Your love. Give me the stamina to stand firm, the grace to hope again, and the faith to know You will never leave me. Amen.

*W*hat then shall we say to this? If God is for us, who is against us? . . . In all these things we are more than conquerors through him who loved us. For I am sure that neither death, nor life, nor angels, nor principalities, nor things present, nor things to come, nor powers, nor height, nor depth, nor anything else in all creation, will be able to separate us from the love of God in Christ Jesus our Lord.

— Romans 8:31, 37-39
(Revised Standard Version)

Daily Reflection

Why is discouragement a spiritual peril? When am I most likely to experience discouragement?

What emotions (defeat, despair, poor self-image, frustration, etc.) do I experience when I am discouraged? What can I do to combat them?

- Elisabeth Leseur says that prayer "upholds us" in times of discouragement. Have I found this to be true in my own life? When? It can be difficult to pray when discouraged. Why must I act "against my will" in this case and pray all the more earnestly?

- St. Vincent de Paul says that God permits these kinds of moments to help us practice two great virtues — "perseverance, which will bring us to our goal" and "steadfastness, which overcomes the difficulties on the way." Looking back over my life, how have they helped me to weather the storm of discouragement? What benefit have they brought?

- Prayerfully read Romans 8 in its entirety. List all of the ways in which God is faithful in the midst of trial and discouragement. What are my nagging worries? List them. How does this passage speak to me about them? How does this bring me hope?

How do discouragement and worry conflict with my mission of spiritual motherhood?

The Peril of Suffering

"Trees that grow in shady and sheltered places, while externally they develop with a healthy appearance, become soft and yielding, and they are easily damaged by anything at all; whereas trees that grow on the tops of very high mountains, buffeted by strong winds and constantly exposed to all types of weather, agitated by storms and frequently covered by snow, become stronger than iron."

St. John Chrysostom

Dear Lord,

Through Baptism I gained entrance into the Paschal Mystery — Your passion, death, and resurrection. And so, the question should not be "Will I suffer?" but rather, "What will I do when I suffer?" Through Your sacrificial offering on Calvary, You have provided me with the grace to endure life's trials and tribulations. You have given me the grace to grow strong amid sufferings and persecutions. You have

*even shown me that joy and peace can be mine despite
contradictions and misunderstandings, reversals and losses.
Give me the grace to embrace my crosses and to unite them
to Your sufferings. Help me to experience the sweet flow of
redemptive grace and the ultimate power of Your resurrection. May my trials be efficacious in my life and in the lives
of others. Amen.*

Scripture Passage for Meditation

My brothers, consider it a great joy when trials of many kinds come upon you, for you well know that the testing of your faith produces perseverance, and perseverance must complete its work so that you will become fully developed, complete, not deficient in any way. . . . Blessed is anyone who perseveres when trials come. Such a person is

of proven worth and will win the
prize of life, the crown that the Lord
has promised to those who love him.

— James 1:2-4, 12
(The New Jerusalem Bible)

Daily Reflection

How can suffering become a spiritual peril?

Consider St. John Chrysostom's quote. What
benefits does suffering bring? St. Augustine
says, "Our pilgrimage on earth cannot be exempt
from trial. We progress by means of trial." To
what extent have I grown in virtue, in faith, and
in trust of God in the midst of trials? Be specific.
What does the Scripture passage tell us about
the benefits of trials — what virtue do they
cultivate? What spiritual benefits? Have I
experienced this in my own life? When and
how? Can sufferings, then, be a cause of
rejoicing?

- Read the passion of Jesus in Mark 14:32-72, 15:1-41. Write down the words that describe His emotional and psychological suffering. Can I identify my own pain and suffering in His? How can I take the grace of Redemption and the power of the Resurrection and apply them to my suffering?

- By uniting our sufferings to the passion of Jesus Christ, many graces can be obtained for me and for others. Pope John Paul II tells us: "It was on Calvary that Mary's suffering beside the suffering Jesus reached an intensity which can hardly be imagined from a human point of view, but which was mysteriously and supernaturally fruitful for the Redemption of the world" (*Salvifici Doloris*). How can my suffering, united to the suffering of Jesus, aid in the redemption of the world? How does this fit with my call of spiritual motherhood?

Section Six

the soul

of woman must be

empty of itself . . .

in order that extraneous

life may have room in it

Section Theme

Woman's soul is a shelter for others.

Section Grace

Pray for the grace to be empty of self that others may find a home in you.

To Seek, To Embrace, To Bring Life

―――――――――――――――――――

"Woman naturally seeks to embrace that which is living, personal, and whole. To cherish, guard, protect, nourish and advance growth is her natural, maternal yearning."

ST. EDITH STEIN

Dear Lord,

The womb of my heart longs to be filled with You. For it is in You and through You only that I can nurture others to spiritual life. Lord, make my heart fertile and ready. Empty it of vanities and attachments. Strip it of pride and self-seeking. Rid it of useless ambitions and attachments. Bless me with receptivity, trust, and surrender. Penetrate me with Your love. Impregnate me with Your life. Nurture other souls to life through me. Amen.

❧❧❧❧❧❧❧❧❧❧❧❧❧❧❧

It is now no longer I that live, but Christ lives in me. And the life that I now live in the flesh, I live in the faith of the Son of God. . . .

— Galatians 2:20
(Challoner-Rheims)

Daily Reflection

❧ St. Edith Stein says that "the soul of woman must be empty of itself in order that extraneous life may have room in it." And, Blessed Mary Magdalene of Martinengo tells us, "By this emptying of self a creature will share more fully in the holiness of God." What is the relationship between emptying of self to holiness, and holiness to the ability to nurture others to life?

❧ In the everyday circumstances of my life, how do I see myself seeking "to embrace that which is living, personal, and whole"? To what extent do

I "cherish, guard, protect, nourish, and advance growth"? How do I do this?

🕊 In what areas of my feminine call as outlined by St. Edith Stein do I feel most adept? Where do I feel weakest? Am I willing to embrace Christ in those weak areas so that I might experience His strength? What are some practical ways that I can do this?

🕊 How can these feminine characteristics begin to transform today's culture and society? How can I communicate this to other women?

Faithful and True

"Mary's transparent openness was the result of her luminous intrepid faith. It never faltered, wavered, or doubted anything that God asked of her. Today we need women of valiant faith who, like Mary, will look upon the fulfillment of God's will in loving trustfulness as the most important accomplishment of their lives."

SISTER MARY ELISE KRANTZ, S.N.D.

Dear Lord,

I consider our Blessed Mother's openness to You. Nothing stood in her way — no stain of sin, no self-seeking, no doubts, no misconceptions or predetermined notions. Free, more free than any human person has ever been and will ever be, she chose You, and You filled her with Your life. Make me like my Mother. Overshadow me with Your Holy Spirit and give me the gift of faith, the gift of trust, the gift of surrender. Show me Your will and give me the fortitude to accomplish it in my life. Let my soul become transparent and open, luminous with faith, a beacon of light that leads your children from the storm-battered shores of life to the safe harbor of Your love. Amen.

Scripture Passage for Meditation

Behold, I am the handmaid of the Lord; let it be to me according to your word.

— Luke 1:38
(Revised Standard Version)

Daily Reflection

Sister Krantz says Mary's "transparent openness" was the result of her "luminous faith." What is the relationship between openness (receptivity) and faith? Consider the use of the words "transparent" and "luminous." What do these adjectives suggest?

In light of this description of Mary's faith, how does my own faith and trust in God compare? Would I describe my receptivity as "transparent"? Why or why not? What relationship, if any, does this have to my motivations for doing God's will?

Sister Krantz suggests that today the world needs women of "valiant faith." What does this mean? Would I describe my faith as "valiant"? What contemporary cultural conditions require "valiant faith"? What faith response would be appropriate?

Determining God's will in light of our feminine mission can be a challenge. Refer to the Appendix and read "Seven Criteria for Discerning God's Will." Have any of these criteria held true in my own life? Am I currently seeking God's will for something particular? Use these seven criteria as an aid to discovery.

The Global Heart of Woman

"For the heart of woman, of every woman, is potentially as vast as the world, since its nature is to envelop all human and created reality. A spontaneous, essentially limitless cosmic sympathy is . . . a property of the feminine consciousness."

LOUIS BOUYER

Dear Lord,

In Your divine design You have created woman to be open, receptive, and embracing. But so much can prevent us from doing so — wounds of the past, personal sins, misunderstanding about what it truly means to receive. Help me to understand this openness and receptivity as it relates to my feminine nature. Show me how to trust, how to surrender, how to accept vulnerability. Make my heart vast enough that all humanity can find a home in it. May my heart be a fount of Your love. Amen.

Scripture Passage for Meditation

*F*or in her is a spirit intelligent, holy, unique, manifold, subtle, mobile, clear, unpolluted, distinct, invulnerable, loving the good, keen, irresistible, beneficent, humane, steadfast, sure, free from anxiety. . . . For Wisdom . . . makes . . . them friends of God. . . .

— Wisdom 7:22-23, 27
(Revised Standard Version)

Daily Reflection

Is my heart open and receptive or is it closed and constricted? To answer, consider the following: Where do I emotionally feel the most vulnerable? What fears do I harbor? In what areas of my life do I exert control? Do I place personal goals above God's will? Do I seek my own comfort level or am I willing to risk?

The soul of woman must be *empty of itself* **159**

❧ Why are trust, surrender, and vulnerability important in my relationship with God? Why are they important in my relationship with others?

❧ The attributes listed from Wisdom are a call to action. Which of these virtues can I identify in myself? What other talents and gifts do I possess? Have I laid them at the service of God for the upbuilding of the Body of Christ?

❧ Which of the attributes from Wisdom do I need to acquire? List a practical strategy for implementing the one quality I most need to exemplify at this time.

❧ How do the above virtues aid in making my heart vast enough "to envelop all human reality"?

The Womb of Woman's Heart

"... Woman's soul is ... fashioned to be a shelter in which other souls may unfold. Both spiritual companionship and spiritual motherliness are not limited to the physical spouse and mother relationships, but they extend to all people with whom woman comes into contact."

St. Edith Stein

Dear Lord,

True friendship is rare. And yet, by my very nature as woman, you call me to be "friend," a gift of self-donation to others. Show me how to acquire loyalty, confidentiality, sincerity, and love. Give me the grace to be selfless, ordering my thoughts, words, and deeds to the benefit of others rather than to myself. Give me the grace to be open and welcoming to the souls You bring to me; help me to see You in them and to rejoice in the revelation. In turn, may I be a reflection of Your love and mercy, and may I make a difference in the world through spiritual companionship and true friendship. May I be that shelter in which other souls may unfold. Amen.

Scripture Passage for Meditation

A faithful friend is a sure shelter, whoever finds one has found a rare treasure. A faithful friend is something beyond price, there is no measuring his worth. A faithful friend is the elixir of life, and those who fear the Lord will find one. Whoever fears the Lord makes true friends, for as a man is, so is his friend.

— Sirach 6:14-17
(The Jerusalem Bible)

Daily Reflection

🍃 Consider the purpose and qualities of a shelter. What do these tell me about the characteristics of a woman's soul? Why is her soul a fitting shelter in which other souls can unfold? Do I have these attributes? Which do I need? How can I acquire them? What do they have to do with friendship and spiritual companionship?

🍃 Who are the women who have been good friends and spiritual companions to me? What virtue did each exhibit that was most life-giving for me? Most life-sustaining? Compose a prayer thanking God for each of these good women.

🍃 What qualities about myself help me to be a "self-donating" person? What qualities work against this good? How can I be a better friend and spiritual companion to my family members and to others? What are some practical strategies I can implement?

🍃 "For as a man is, so is his friend." What does this passage indicate about the importance of a good

example? Would I want others to imitate me?
Why or why not? In what ways do I need to
improve my example?

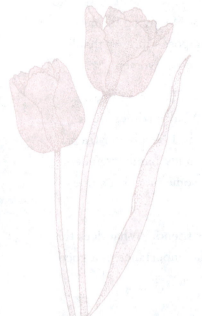

The Profit of Woman's Soul

"Woman's soul will profit only if it goes abroad to *search* and to bring home the hidden *treasure* which rests in every human soul, and which can enrich not only her soul but also others; and it will profit only if it searches and bears home the well-known or hidden *burden* which is laid on every human soul . . . and its expanses *must* widen in order to be able to take in what it carries."

ST. EDITH STEIN

Dear Lord,

You have created the feminine heart to see the good in others and You have created the feminine soul to be a refuge and safe haven for those in need. But sometimes my heart is too crowded with my own concerns to give space to others. Empty my heart, Lord, and fill it with Your love. Help my heart to be a shelter with enough room for all those whom You bring to me. May they experience Your life in me and thus be brought to life in You. Amen.

Scripture Passage for Meditation

*A*nd Simeon blessed them, and said to Mary his mother, "Behold, this child is destined for the fall and for the rise of many in Israel, and for a sign that shall be contradicted. And thy own soul a sword shall pierce, that the thoughts of many hearts may be revealed."

— Luke 2:34-35
(Challoner-Rheims)

Daily Reflection

Do I "search for the hidden treasure" within the people who populate my life (consider home life, work life, and leisure) or am I quick to point out their faults and failings? Am I receptive to those in need?

- Do I strive to make myself available to those who may need a motherly heart?

- St. Thérèse of Lisieux says that "a word, a kindly smile, will often suffice to gladden a wounded and sorrowful heart." Today, commit to "nurture" at least three people in this way — a family member, a friend or acquaintance, a complete stranger. At day's end, record the experience, its effect on you personally, and its effect on the other person (if known).

- Simeon tells the Blessed Virgin that a sword will pierce her soul so that the thoughts of many may be revealed. Read 2 Corinthians 1:4. What area of my heart has been deeply wounded? How can my own suffering become a source of consolation for others?

A Heart Open to All

"Those who are separated from us by birth, education, belief, . . . those who are most abject and most guilty — all are entitled to our love. . . . Do they not all stand before God, beloved by Him? Has not each a soul like our own? . . . Let us open our hearts to admit all humanity. At the touch of the divine let us resound with every gracious thought, every human affection. . . ."

ELISABETH LESEUR

Dear Lord,

Am I willing to be a spiritual mother to everyone? Even as I prayerfully ask the question, I know the answer. The horrible truth is that my heart is too narrow to permit every person an entrance. Prejudice binds me. Biases restrict me. Bigotry chains me. Transform me, O Lord. Heal me, O Lord. Renew me, O Lord. For only Your love can open my heart, only Your love can broaden its expanse, only Your love active within me can gain everyone an entrance. Amen.

$\mathcal{S}$trip off the old man with his deeds and put on the new, one that is being renewed unto perfect knowledge "according to the image of his Creator." Here there is not "Gentile and Jew," "circumcised and uncircumcised," "Barbarian and Scythian," "slave and freeman" but Christ is all things and in all.

— Colossians 3:9-10
(Challoner-Rheims)

Daily Reflection

Refer to the Appendix and read the selection. Name three new ideas that were presented to me in this section. How can they positively influence my thinking? To what extent can I share them with others?

🌿 To what extent do I respect the image of God in everyone I meet — even the most unsavory?

🌿 What groups of people commonly experience prejudice? Have I myself been the target of prejudice? Recall the incident. How did it make me feel?

🌿 Do prejudices and biases prevent me from being open to all of God's children (consider race, ethnic background, creed, socioeconomic status, age groups)? If yes, name them. What practical strategies can I employ to overcome my bigotry?

🌿 Why is prejudicial treatment (for or against) a sin? How have we as a culture sinned in this way? How have I personally sinned in this way? How does this impact on the call of spiritual motherhood?

Love for All Eternity

"Mothers of children, even if they have a thousand children, carry each and every one fixed in their hearts, and because of the strength of their love they do not forget any of them. . . . Surely those who are mothers in spirit can and must act all the more in the same way, because spiritual love is more powerful than the love that comes from a blood relationship."

ST. ANGELA MERICI

Dear Lord,

You have placed many souls into my heart. Give me the grace to nurture them with Your love, to encourage them with the truths of Your Church, to intercede for them with faithfulness of heart. Help me never to forget my responsibility toward them. And should progress seem slow and transformation long in coming, give me the trust, the perseverance, and the hope I need to know that "for those who love God all things work together unto good, for those who, according to His purpose, are saints through His call." Amen.

Scripture Passage for Meditation

೧೪೨೧೪೨೧೪೨೧೪೨೧೪೨೧೪೨೧

Can a woman forget her baby at the breast, feel no pity for the child she has borne? Even if these were to forget, I shall not forget you. Look, I have engraved you on the palms of my hands. . . .

— Isaiah 49:15-16
(The New Jerusalem Bible)

Daily Reflection

❧ Who are the spiritual children whom God has entrusted to me? Make a list of them. What are their special needs? Write their needs next to their names. How can I spiritually "mother" them according to their needs?

Go to the Appendix and read the excerpt from *Lumen Gentium* about the Blessed Mother.

1. In this passage many attributes of the Blessed Virgin Mary are given. List them — both those that are stated and those that are implied.

2. When did Mary's "spiritual motherhood" begin? When will it end?

3. What does it mean by "until the eternal fulfillment of all the elect"?

4. Consider this passage in light of St. Angela Merici's quotation. How do the two relate? Consider it in light of the Scripture passage. How do the two relate?

5. How does this excerpt reveal Mary's spiritual motherhood?

6. What does it tell me about the mission of spiritual motherhood?

Section Seven

the soul

of woman must be

mistress of itself . . .

so that the entire person is

readily at the disposal

of every call

Section Theme

Women have an essential mission in the world.

Section Grace

Pray for the grace to effect change in the world through the gift of authentic femininity and the grace of spiritual motherhood.

Called and Gifted: Woman in the World

"The hour is coming, in fact has come, when the vocation of woman is being acknowledged in its fullness, the hour in which women acquire in the world an influence, an effect and a power never hitherto achieved. That is why, at this moment when the human race is undergoing so deep a transformation, women impregnated with a spirit of the Gospel can do so much to aid humanity in not falling."

POPE PAUL VI

Dear Lord,

Impregnate me with the spirit of the Gospel and let me bring Your life to the world. I want to birth You in the lives of the poor, the downtrodden, the weak and maligned. I want to birth You in the hearts of the fearful, the distraught, the grief-stricken and desolate. I want to birth You in the souls of the wounded, the troubled, the lonely, the bereft. I want to birth You to the proud, the arrogant, the sophisticated, and the chic. I want to birth You in moments of pain and confusion, doubt and disillusion, trial and travail. I want to birth You in abortuaries and prison cells, in research labs and legislative caucuses. I want to birth You in grade schools and high schools, in college classes and think-tank sessions. I want to birth You in my family and parish, my community and country. The hour has come. Let my labor begin. May Your life infuse the world. Amen.

Scripture Passage for Meditation

I do not cease to give thanks for you, remembering you in my prayers, that the God of our Lord Jesus Christ, the Father of glory, may give you a spirit of wisdom and of revelation in the knowledge of him, having the eyes of your hearts enlightened, that you may know what is the hope to which he has called you, . . . and what is the immeasurable greatness of his power in us who believe.

— Ephesians 1:15-19
(Revised Standard Version)

Daily Reflection

🌿 What does it mean to be "impregnated with a spirit of the Gospel"? How does this occur? What personal steps have I taken to be "impregnated with the Gospel spirit"? How have I nurtured this spirit within me?

🌿 What power and influence do women have at this time in the history of mankind that has never been achieved before? How can women who are "impregnated with the spirit of the Gospel" become transforming agents in the world? How could this impact on the culture of the day? According to the Scripture passage, what is the extent of this power in believers?

- What special gifts does St. Paul tell us we are receiving for our mission? Why are they necessary? Have they been operative in me? How?

- What areas of contemporary life need to be transformed? In what ways is "humanity falling"? What can I personally do to effect change in these areas? How can I do this on a personal and individual level?

- St. Thérèse of Lisieux said, "Suffering alone gives birth to souls." The birthing process is painful. What kinds of pain can I expect if I set out to birth Jesus Christ to the world? Am I willing to endure it? Why or why not? What can I do to prepare for it?

The Transforming Power of Intercessory Prayer

"I believe in the power of prayers. . . . I believe in them because God exists, and because He is the Father. I believe in them because I believe in the divine and mysterious law that we call the Communion of Saints. I know that no cry, no desire, no appeal proceeding from the depths of our soul is lost, but all go to God and through Him to those who move us to pray."

ELISABETH LESEUR

Dear Lord,

So much can happen through prayer! Scripture tells me that the prayers of the righteous accomplish much. I think of Abraham's intercession for Sodom and Gomorrah. I think of Moses' intercession for the Israelites. I think of Mary's intercession at the wedding feast in Cana. And I think of Your own intercession for Your followers before Your passion and death. Help me to accept my mission of intercession. Help me to persevere, to stand firm, and to trust in You. Help me to remember that You desire to meet the needs of this world more than I desire for You to meet those needs. May my prayers bring life to those I love and life to the world. Amen.

Scripture Passage for Meditation

A sk and it will be given you; seek, and you will find; knock, and it will be opened to you. For everyone who asks receives, and he who seeks finds, and to him who knocks it will be opened.

— Matthew 7:7-8
(Revised Standard Version)

Daily Reflection

🌿 Elisabeth Leseur said that she believed in the power of prayers. Do I? Refer to the following Scripture passages: James 5:16, Genesis 18:16-33, Exodus 32. What do these passages tell me about the power of intercessory prayer? Look at the passages from Genesis and Exodus. How do current cultural conditions parallel with the cultural conditions referred to? What can I learn about intercessory prayer from Abraham and Moses?

🌿 Intercessory prayer can transform lives, relationships, situations, and world events. Following are five key actions that define an effective intercessor. How many of them do I have? Am I willing to work in the areas where I am weak?

1. The effective intercessor accepts the mission.
2. The effective intercessor is one who perseveres.
3. The effective intercessor guards herself against personal sin.

4. The effective intercessor practices humility through sacrifice.

5. The effective intercessor desires the will of God.

(From *Full of Grace: Women and the Abundant Life*)

🍂 Read about the wedding feast at Cana (John 2:1-11). How does each characteristic of the effective intercessor apply to the Blessed Mother?

🍂 To transform the world, each of us needs to be an intercessor in our personal lives and in our communal lives. Pray for the guidance of the Holy Spirit. For whom is God asking me to intercede? For what circumstance is He asking me to intercede? For what cultural or world situation is God asking me to intercede? Using the five key actions of an effective intercessor, make a commitment to intercede daily for these intentions.

Transforming Deeds

"Miss no single opportunity of making some small sacrifice, here by a smiling look, there by a kindly word; always doing the smallest thing right, and doing it all for love. . . . True charity consists in putting up with all one's neighbor's faults, never being surprised by his weakness, and being inspired by the least of his virtues."

ST. THÉRÈSE OF LISIEUX

Dear Lord,

Great apostolic works are comprised of faithfully executing our everyday activities with the love of Christ. And, this is also how we grow in holiness and grace. Help me to respond to all of life's contradictions with joy, hope, and forbearance. Help me to respond to each individual with love, peace, and self-control. Help me to remember that it is not how much I do for You, but rather, how faithfully and lovingly I do it. May my little deeds of love become channels of grace through which Your life comes into the world. Amen.

Scripture Passage for Meditation

*A*nd let us not grow weary in well doing, for in due season we shall reap, if we do not lose heart. So then, as we have opportunity, let us do good to all men, and especially to those who are of the household of faith.

— Galatians 6:9-10
(Revised Standard Version)

Daily Reflection

Transforming the world often begins with individual acts of kindness and Christian charity. Read the account written by St. Thérèse of Lisieux in the Appendix. Then contemplate these questions:

1. What practical strategies did St. Thérèse employ to act with charity toward the nun

who distressed her so? What indications suggest this was not always easy?

2. What effect did her charitable actions have? What tells us they "warmed the heart" of the offending nun? How was this action one of spiritual motherhood? Did St. Thérèse's actions lead her to a change of heart regarding this nun — what suggests so?

3. St. Thérèse exhibited heroic virtue. What were the virtues she displayed? How does the passage from Galatians encourage me to do the same? How will these same virtues help me to effect change in today's culture and the world community?

4. Can I identify my "pet peeves"? In my life, who demonstrates them? How can these become opportunities for me to grow in holiness? To fulfill my mission of spiritual motherhood? Ask St. Thérèse for her intercession to act with heroic virtue.

Transforming Love

"To learn from the Heart of Jesus the secret of love for souls and deep knowledge of them: how to touch their hurts without making them smart and to dress their wounds without reopening them; to give oneself to them and yet reserve oneself; to disclose Truth in its entirety and yet to make it known according to the degree of light that each soul can bear. The knowledge required for the apostolate can be had only from Jesus Christ, by encountering Him in the Eucharist and in prayer."

ELISABETH LESEUR

Dear Lord,

In Scripture You give us the story of the Good Samaritan. How carefully he tends the wounds of the one he finds lying half-dead. With what love and compassion he makes provision for him. How honorable and Christ-like are his actions. Help me to be like the Good Samaritan. Give me the courage to tend the spiritual wounds of my neighbor, to dress the wounds of his heart with the balm of charity, to make provision for him through prayer and mortification. May I be a reflection of Your love in his life. Amen.

I tell you most solemnly, whoever believes in me will perform the same works as I do myself, he will perform even greater works, because I am going to the Father. Whatever you ask for in my name I will do, so that the Father may be glorified in the Son.

— John 13:12-13
(The Jerusalem Bible)

Daily Reflection

🕊 One spiritual writer says that we are all "wounded healers." How have I been a "wounded healer"? Are there wounds I fear exposing to others or myself? How could these "hidden" wounds prevent me from ministering to others' needs?

🕊 Which of the feminine attributes and virtues are most necessary for this spiritual work of mercy? What are some ordinary ways that this mission is presented to me daily?

🕊 Good listening skills help equip us for "dressing the wounds" of others. What qualities distinguish a good listener? Do I have these? Which must I develop?

🕊 Elisabeth Leseur says that we must learn from the heart of Jesus "to disclose truth in its entirety and yet to make it known according to the degree of light that each soul can bear."

1. How can I speak the truth about difficult issues in a loving and compassionate way?

2. How does this kind of tender regard nurture both the heart and the soul of the one whom I counsel?

3. How does speaking the truth lead to spiritual healing?

Mortification is a powerful spiritual tool. How can mortification become a "dressing" for the wounds of others? In what ways can I practice mortification for this purpose?

The Transforming Effect of Good Example

"Good example is the most efficacious apostolate; you must be as lighted lanterns and shine like brilliant chandeliers among men. By your good example and your words, animate others to know and love God."

ST. MARY JOSEPH ROSSELLO

Dear Lord,

I want to be a brilliant prism that reflects Your love to the world! May the witness of my life bring others to life — a life marked by generosity, gentleness, self-giving, surrender. Let me radiate compassion, joy, peace, and faith. May my every word and every action speak of hope, healing, and eternal happiness. I pray that through me, many others may come to know the abundant life that You offer. Amen.

❧❧❧❧❧❧❧❧❧❧❧❧❧❧

*Y*ou are the light of the world. A city set on a hill cannot be hid. Nor do men light a lamp and put it under a bushel, but on a stand, and it gives light to all in the house. Let your light so shine before men, that they may see your good works and give glory to your Father who is in heaven.

— Matthew 5:14-16
(Revised Standard Version)

Daily Reflection

🙠 Am I comfortable with the idea that my words and actions influence others? Why or why not?

🙠 In what ways am I a "light" for others?

🙠 The example of the Blessed Mother's life leads others to holiness and conformity to God's will. To what extent am I influencing others in this same direction (my spouse, my children, my friends, my colleagues)? Think of specific examples and illustrations from daily life.

🖋 Daily prayer, the Holy Mass, and the sacraments are the "oil" that makes my "lamp" shine. How do they act as a catalyst for light? To what extent do I take advantage of the grace available to me through these means? Do I need to improve my efforts? In what ways?

🖋 Faithful reception of the Eucharist and adoration of the Blessed Sacrament fill us with the light of Jesus Christ. Read 2 Corinthians 3:17-18. What does this passage tell me about "gazing on the Lord's glory"? How can this transforming effect in me become a transforming effect in others? What "veils" may hide my face from the Lord's glory? How can I remove them to receive even more of His light?

Blossoms of a Fruitful Effort

"We pray, suffer, and labor in ignorance of the consequence of our acts and prayers. God makes them serve His supreme plan; gradually they take their effect, winning one soul, then another. They hasten the coming of the Kingdom of God and by the other beings, acts, and desires they give birth to, they will exert an influence that will endure until the end of time."

ELISABETH LESEUR

Dear Lord,

In this life I may never fully appreciate how You have used my words, my prayers, and my sacrifices to lead others to You. But I know that everything offered to You yields fruit for the Kingdom. Let the witness of my life be an instrument in Your hands. Use me as an instrument of transformation in today's world. May I warm the hearts of others, nurture them to spiritual life, and sustain them in knowledge of You. And, may they, in turn, become catalysts of holy love, drawing still others to You, until that glorious day when we shall be with You forever in heaven. Amen.

Scripture Passage for Meditation

I accommodated myself to people in all kinds of different situations, so that by all possible means I might bring some to salvation. All this I do for the sake of the gospel, that I may share its benefits with others.

— 1 Corinthians 9:22-23
(The New Jerusalem Bible)

Daily Reflection

- Specifically, in what ways have I prayed, suffered, and labored for the salvation of others?

- Have I "accommodated myself to people in all kinds of different situations" so that some might come to salvation? Consider different age groups of people, various areas of service in which I am involved, life circumstances in which others may find themselves. In what particular ways have I accommodated myself?

❧ Refer to the Appendix and read the additional quote by Elisabeth Leseur. To what extent do I consciously strive to be an "attractive" witness of the Gospel message? Do I exhibit the fruits of devotion, charity, and radiant faith? Which of the "flowers" listed do I present to others? Which can I work to develop?

❧ Sometimes God permits us to see the fruit of our labors to encourage us in our mission of spiritual motherhood. What are some moments from my life when my personal "accommodations," "attractiveness," "fruit," and "flowers" yielded a harvest? To what extent did they encourage me in my mission of spiritual maternity?

The Transforming Effect of Woman in the Modern World

". . . Every woman without exception is under an obligation — a strict obligation of conscience, mind you! — not to remain aloof; every woman must go into action, each in her own way, and join in stemming the tides which threaten to engulf the home, in fighting the doctrines which undermine its foundations, in preparing, organizing, and completing its restoration."

POPE PIUS XII

Dear Lord,

These are strong words spoken by Pope Pius XII! And they prick my conscience. I have excused myself from becoming involved and I have used a variety of reasons to justify my position of remaining "aloof." Help me to overcome my fears, my reticence, my sense of inadequacy. Help me to overcome my pride, my complacency, my laziness. Give me the courage to step with confidence and assurance into the situations that present themselves to me. Give me the conviction and holy zeal necessary to tackle the greater issues of our culture and society — issues that threaten human life, family life, spiritual life. May I be a conduit of grace through which Your life flows into the world. May I be an instrument of transformation. Amen.

Scripture Passage for Meditation

If my people who are called by my name humble themselves, and pray and seek my face, and turn from their wicked ways, then I will hear from heaven, and will forgive their sin and heal their land. Now my eyes will be open and my ears attentive to the prayer made in this place.

— 2 Chronicles 7:14
(Revised Standard Version)

Daily Reflection

🕊 What forces and/or doctrines are currently a threat to the social and moral well-being of family life, human life, and spiritual life? To what extent do I feel "a strict obligation of conscience" to "go into action" against them?

🕊 Pope Pius XII says each woman must go into action "each in her own way." What are some ways that women can go into action? Considering my gifts, talents, preferences, and personality, of these ways, which is "my way"? How can I move forward in this way? What does it require of me? Prepare a "plan of engagement." How can preparation and organization support my apostolic efforts?

🕊 According to 2 Chronicles 7:14, healing and restoration of our country and culture must begin with me. In what specific ways? How does this concept fit in with the notion of "social sin" as discussed previously in "A Communion of Sin" (under Section Four)? How does it relate to the notion of "social good" as discussed in this same section?

❧ How is Christian social action in keeping with the call to spiritual motherhood?

Section Eight

the soul

of woman . . .

Mary and the

feminine ideal

Section Theme
The Blessed Mother is the perfect model of the feminine ideal.

Section Grace
Pray for the grace to become a daughter of Mary.

The Ideal Woman

"Yes, Christian women, the future of civil society and of the ecclesial community expects much of your sensitivity and of your capacity for understanding, of your sweetness and of your perseverance, of your generosity and of your humility. These virtues — so well in accord with feminine psychology and magnificently developed in the Virgin Mary — are also the fruits of the Holy Spirit. This Holy Spirit will guide you. . . ."

POPE PAUL VI

Hail Mary, full of grace, the Lord is with thee; blessed art thou among women, and blessed is the fruit of thy womb, Jesus.

Holy Mary, Mother of God, pray for us sinners, now and at the hour of our death. Amen.

rise, shine; for your light has come, and the glory of the Lord has risen upon you. For behold, darkness shall cover the earth, and thick darkness the peoples; but the Lord will arise upon you, and his glory will be seen upon you. And nations shall come to your light, and kings to the brightness of your rising. Lift up your eyes round about, and see; they all gather together, they come to you; your sons shall come from far, and your daughters shall be carried in the arms. Then you shall see and be radiant, your heart shall thrill and rejoice; . . .

— Isaiah 60:1-5
(Revised Standard Version)

Daily Reflection

🍂 How is the Scripture passage a word about the Blessed Mother? How is it a word to the women of our day and time? Specifically, how is it a word for me? What is my response?

🍂 The Blessed Virgin Mary is the exemplar of the perfect disciple and the ideal woman. Use these Scripture passages — Luke 1:26-38; Luke 1:39-45, 56; Luke 1:46-55; Luke 2:33-35, 51; Matthew 2:13-15; John 2:1-12; John 19:25-27 — to form the basis of your prayer time for the next few days. Pray the Hail Mary, then reflect on the following questions for each of the passages:

1. What spiritual quality of the Blessed Mother does the Scripture passage illustrate? What fruit of the Holy Spirit (see Galatians 5:22)? How are these in accord with feminine psychology and the mission of spiritual motherhood?

2. In what ways do mankind and our contemporary culture need this quality and this fruit of the Holy Spirit?

3. How do I see myself imitating this quality of the Blessed Virgin in my own life? How does this help me in my mission of spiritual motherhood?

4. Pope Paul VI says that the Holy Spirit will guide us in our quest of spiritual motherhood. Using the Scripture passages as my basis, how do I see the Holy Spirit interacting in the life of the Blessed Virgin Mary? How have I seen Him intervening in my life? Why is His guidance necessary for our spiritual call?

The Soul of Woman: A Final Reflection

"The soul of a woman must . . . be expansive and open to all human beings; it must be quiet so that no small weak flame will be extinguished by stormy winds; warm so as not to benumb fragile buds; clear, so that no vermin will settle in dark corners and recesses; self-contained, so that no invasions from without can peril the inner life; empty of itself, in order that extraneous life may have room in it; finally, mistress of itself and also of its body, so that the entire person is readily at the disposal of every call."

St. Edith Stein

Dear Lord,

Throughout this study You have shown me so much about what it means to be woman. You have shown me that my essential mission is to bring others to spiritual life, to nurture them in their relationship with You, to help them grow strong in the Faith and in Your life. This is accomplished by my call to spiritual motherhood, a call You have ordained for me from all eternity and a call accomplished through the gift of authentic femininity.

You have shown me that women, impregnated with a spirit of the Gospel, can change the course of the world and the destiny of mankind; and, You have shown me that to be impregnated with You, I must seek a holy life steeped in prayer, the sacraments, renunciation of vices, and growth in virtue.

You have shown me that now is the time for me to step into the fullness of my womanhood, and You encouraged me to do so with fortitude, commitment, and conviction. You have shown me that at this moment, the world desperately needs my gift of spiritual motherhood, and that my witness of faith will aid humanity in not falling. And, You have strengthened me to persevere in times of tribulation and stress, trial and misunderstanding, confusion and contradiction.

Lord, to strengthen me in my womanhood, You have given me the Blessed Virgin Mary as my model. Inspired by *her total act of self-donation, I pray for the gift of receptiv-ity, the gift of trust, and the gift of surrender. I pray for an open heart, a fertile soul, and a spirit pregnant with Your divine life. May she make intercession for me as I seek to be a woman full of grace in today's culture. And, may I one day stand with her in Your heavenly kingdom, a daughter who continues to bring Your life to the world. Amen.*

Scripture Passage for Meditation

The Spirit of the Lord is upon me, because the Lord has anointed me to bring good tidings to the afflicted; he has sent me to bind up the brokenhearted, to proclaim liberty to the captives, and the opening of the prison to those who are bound; to proclaim the year of the Lord's favor, and the day of vengeance of our God; to comfort all who mourn; to grant to those who mourn in Zion —

to give them a garland instead of ashes,
the oil of gladness instead of mourning,
the mantle of praise instead of a faint
spirit; that they may be called oaks of
righteousness, the planting of the Lord,
that he may be glorified. They shall build
up ancient ruins, they shall raise up the
former devastations; they shall repair the
ruined cities, the devastations of many
generations.

— Isaiah 61:1-4
(Revised Standard Version)

Daily Reflection

In what specific ways has my concept of womanhood changed as a result of my prayer and
reflection through the last several weeks?

To what extent have I embraced my call to
spiritual motherhood? How am I living it more
fully now than when I began *Grace-Filled
Moments*? In what ways has my awareness of

spiritual motherhood transformed my everyday attitudes toward life and its circumstances?

🌿 What do I see as my particular spheres of "spiritual-motherly" influence? Have I sensed the Lord expanding the borders of my spheres? Where may He be calling me? To what extent am I willing to accept the challenge?

🌿 What are the various "missions" expressed in the Scripture passage? How are these missions in conformity to my call to spiritual motherhood? Notice the last sentence of the passage. What does it tell us will be the outcome of living the mission? How does this apply to the spiritual, emotional, psychological, and cultural life of mankind?

🌿 Will I say "Yes" to my call to be spiritual mother? As a closing exercise, formulate a prayer of commitment to the Lord. Read it each day in your time of prayer as a reminder of Who it is that has chosen you and to what He has called you. May God bless you today and always.

SECTION ONE

Reference for "The Womb of Woman"

(The following is taken from the *Catechism of the Catholic Church.*)

1652—"By its very nature the institution of marriage and married love is ordered to the procreation and education of the offspring and it is in them that it finds its crowning glory" [*GS* 48 § 1; 50].

2363—The spouses' union achieves the twofold end of marriage: the good of the spouses themselves and the transmission of life. These two meanings or values of marriage cannot be separated without altering the couple's spiritual life and compromising the goods of marriage and the future of the family.

The conjugal love of man and woman thus stands under the twofold obligation of fidelity and fecundity.

2366—Fecundity is a gift, an *end of marriage*, for conjugal love naturally tends to be fruitful. A child does not come from outside as something added on to the mutual love of the spouses, but springs from the very heart of that mutual giving, as its fruit and fulfillment. So the church, which "is on the side of life" [*FC* 30] teaches that "it is necessary that each and every marriage act must remain ordered *per se* to the procreation of human life" [*HV* 11]. This particular doctrine, expounded on numerous occasions by the Magisterium, is based on the inseparable connection, established by God, which man on his own initiative may not break, between the unitive significance and the procreative significance which are both inherent to the marriage act" [*HV* 12; cf. Pius XI, encyclical, *Casti connubii*].

2367 — Called to give life, spouses share in the creative power and fatherhood of God [Cf. *Eph* 3:14; *Mt* 23:9]. "Married couples should regard it as their proper mission to transmit human life and to educate their children; they should realize that they are thereby *cooperating with* the love of *God the Creator* and are, in a certain sense, its interpreters. They will fulfill this duty with a sense of human and Christian responsibility" [*GS* 50 § 2].

2368 — A particular aspect of this responsibility concerns the *regulation of procreation*. For just reasons, spouses may wish to space the births of their children. It is their duty to make certain that their desire is not motivated by selfishness but is in conformity with the generosity appropriate to responsible parenthood. Moreover, they should conform their behavior to the objective criteria of morality:

When it is a question of harmonizing married love with the responsible transmission of life, the morality of the behavior does not depend on sincere intention and evaluation of motives alone; but it must be determined by objective criteria, criteria drawn from the nature of the person and his acts, criteria that respect the total meaning of mutual self-giving and human procreation in the context of true love; this is possible only if the virtue of married chastity is practiced with sincerity of heart [GS 51 § 3].

2370—Periodic continence, that is, the methods of birth regulation based on self-observation and the use of infertile periods, is in conformity with the objective criteria of morality [HV 16]. These methods respect the bodies of the spouses, encourage tenderness between them, and favor the education of an authentic freedom. In contrast, "every action which, whether in anticipation of the conjugal act, or in its accomplishment, or in the development of its natural consequences, proposes, whether as an end or as a means, to render procreation impossible" is intrinsically evil [*HV* 14]:

> Thus the innate language that expresses the total reciprocal self-giving of a husband and wife is overlaid, through contraception, by an objectively contradictory language, namely, that of not giving oneself totally to the other. This leads not only to a positive refusal to be open to life but also to a falsification of the inner truth of conjugal love, which is called upon to give itself in personal totality. . . . The difference, both anthropological and moral, between contraception and recourse to the rhythm of the cycle . . . involves in the final analysis two irreconcilable concepts of the human person and of human sexuality [*FC* 32].

Section Two

Reference for "The Perfect Woman"

(The following is taken from the *Catechism of the Catholic Church*.)

2744—*Prayer is a vital necessity.* Proof from the contrary is no less convincing: if we do not allow the Spirit to lead us, we fall back into the slavery of sin [Cf. *Gal* 5:16-25]. How can the Holy Spirit be our life if our heart is far from him?

> Nothing is equal to prayer; for what is impossible it makes possible, what is difficult, easy. . . . For it is impossible, utterly impossible, for the man who prays eagerly and invokes God ceaselessly ever to sin [St. John Chrysostom, *De Anna* 4, 5: PG 54, 666].

> Those who pray are certainly saved; those who do not pray are certainly damned [St. Alphonsus Liguori, *Del gran mezzo della preghiera*].

Reference for "Raising Our Hearts and Minds to God"

(The following is taken from *Full of Grace: Women and the Abundant Life*.)

What Is Prayer?

All prayer is simply a response to God's unconditional love for us and His invitation to experience that love. In prayer, God lifts our hearts and minds to Him as we desire to completely surrender to His action in us. Through prayer, God calls us into intimacy with Him, an intimacy that transforms us, an intimacy that imbues us with His presence, an intimacy that is life-giving. . . . In union with God through prayer, we become a radiant image of His life active in the world, igniting it with the fire of His love.

Vocal Prayer

Vocal prayer is one type of prayer. It can be subdivided into formulated vocal prayer and spontaneous vocal prayer.

Formulated vocal prayer. Formulated prayers use words that have been developed beforehand. Examples include the Hail Mary, the Our Father, the prayers of the Holy Sacrifice of the Mass, the Rosary, and the Liturgy of the Hours. Formulated vocal prayers can be recited alone or with others. These prayers, when offered to God with reverence, devotion, and attention, will stir within us a desire to enter more deeply into the life of God.

A thoughtful, reverent attitude of the heart is of utmost importance when we enter into vocal prayer.

Jesus Himself admonished His disciples on the importance of praying with the heart and not just the mouth: "In praying, do not babble like the pagans, who think that they will be heard because of their many words. Do not be like them" (Matthew 6:7-8, *New American Bible*).

We must evaluate for ourselves whether we are truly praying or simply reciting words. If our desire to grow closer to God is not growing greater, we need to unite ourselves more faithfully to the words we are saying. As we grow in desire for God, our natural yearning will be to spend more time with Him and to come to know Him more intimately. These growing desires for God tell us that our love of Him is deepening and signal that our prayer life is expanding. It is often at this point that we experience the second type of vocal prayer, spontaneous vocal prayer.

Spontaneous vocal prayer. As our love for God grows and develops, we desire to express it to Him in sentiments and emotions which rise up out of our own hearts and minds. These prayers, spoken in our own words, are called spontaneous prayers. Sometimes our spontaneous prayer is expressed in short ejaculations which punctuate our daily activities — *Thank you, Jesus; Have mercy on me, Lord; Dear God, give me patience and grace.* Sometimes it forms the portion of our prayer time when we praise God or thank Him for favors we have received. In group settings like a prayer meeting or a time of praise at a conference, our spontaneous prayer may be joined to that of others.

As we grow more comfortable with spontaneous prayer, we soon desire to spend longer periods of time speaking with God. We want to share with Him our trials and struggles and talk with Him about major decisions to be made. We want to tell Him our true inner thoughts, make Him privy to the deepest parts of our heart, share with Him those areas within us that are broken and need His healing touch. As we pray in this way, we discover that our time with God produces precious fruit: a deep assurance of His great love for us and a growing awareness of our love for Him.

Gradually, our conversation with God becomes less verbal and more interior. Though we still use words to express our thoughts, we notice that our time of prayer becomes marked by lengthening periods of silence as we quietly wait to hear God's voice speaking to us. This is right because our conversation with Him is to be a dialogue, not a monologue. If we are to hear the voice of God whispering within us, we must quiet ourselves. We must cultivate the gift of listening. And, as our listening skills develop, God's voice can be heard deep within our hearts even in the midst of activity and noise.

This interior exchange between us and God is sometimes called *mental prayer.* Mental prayer marks a significant deepening of our prayer experience and leads us along the way of prayer.

As with formulated vocal prayer, spontaneous vocal prayer must engage the mind, the heart, and the will. It does no good to "say" prayers or to make pious and sentimental statements. Our prayers must be defined by a desire to conform all aspects of our being to the movement of God's grace within us. Therefore, in prayer we must be present to God in body, mind, and spirit as He moves us forward to the central reality of a life of faith — Christ living in us. It is this to which we are called. And it is only as God's grace accomplishes this in us that we grow to full stature in Christ Jesus.

Reference for "The Bouquet of Prayer"

(The following is taken from *A Catholic Dictionary.*)

Meditation — The lowest kind of mental prayer, called also discursive prayer. It consists of reflections on a given subject with the practical aim of stirring the will to make acts of faith, love, humility, etc., and to form resolutions. In recent centuries it has become common to have systematized methods of meditation, in order to give direction to one's reflections and ensure more deliberate and determined effort on the part of the will. There are many varieties of such methods, but the two chief are that of St. Ignatius, to be found in his "Spiritual Exercises," and the method of St. Sulpice. . . . Meditation is the prayer of beginners in the spiritual life and is proper to the purgative way. It grows gradually into affective prayer, in which the will requires less assistance from the reflections of the mind, but almost at once begins to make acts of love, humility, etc. Finally, there may come a time when, through no fault of her own, the soul can neither reflect nor make acts. She has fallen into aridity. Yet she truly desires union with God. She is ripe for the prayer of simplicity and should be guided into it. St. John of the Cross speaks severely of directors who in such circumstances would still force the soul to meditate.

Recollection — Another name for two grades of prayer: The Prayer of Simplicity and the Prayer of Quiet.

The Prayer of Simplicity. Called also, of faith, of simple regard, . . . of loving attention. It is the first contemplative prayer. "Meditation is very good in its time, and very useful at the beginning of the spiritual life, but one must not stop there; for by fidelity to mortification and recollection, the soul ordinarily receives a purer and more intimate prayer, which may be called prayer of simplicity and consists in a simple look, regard or loving attention directed towards God himself or one of his mysteries or some other Christian truth. The soul ceases to reason and employs a sweet contemplation which keeps it peaceful, attentive to and susceptible of the divine operations and impressions which the Holy Ghost communicates to it" (Bossuet). . . .

The Prayer of Quiet. The first stage of mystical union is called the state of quietude. Its characteristic prayer is the prayer of quiet. This prayer begins in passive recollection, when the eyes close, the ears cease to attend to outward objects (although they still hear them) and the body remains perfectly still. The imagination, however, is restless and wandering. Then God makes himself felt by the soul in an obscure way as a great Reality or Presence, and the heart reposes in tranquil love of him and is gently permeated with spiritual sweetness, to which sensible devotion bears no comparison. Such delightful prayer is at first of very brief duration, and the habitual condition of the soul is one of arid contemplation. Later, however, it lasts longer until towards the end of the state of quietude, it becomes in a modified form habitual.

Reference for "Loving Those in Our Midst"

The Spiritual Works of Mercy are: to convert sinners, to instruct the ignorant, to counsel the wayward, to comfort the sorrowing, to bear adversity patiently, to forgive offenses, and to pray for the living and the dead.

The Corporal Works of Mercy are: to feed the hungry, to clothe the naked, to give drink to the thirsty, to shelter the homeless, to tend the sick, to visit prisoners, and to bury the dead.

Reference for "Life-Giving Words"

(The following is taken from *Our Moral Life in Christ*.)

Sins Against Another's Reputation

Calumny

Calumny is a lie told about someone, accusing him of something of which he is not guilty. Calumny is what is directly forbidden in the formulation of this precept in the Old Testament where it says: "You shall not bear false witness against your neighbor" (Exodus 20:16; Deuteronomy 5:20).

Everyone has the right to fame and honor. *Fame* is the positive or negative opinion which is commonly held about another person. *Honor* is the testimony of the excellence of a man's character. The sin against a person's fame or honor is called *disparagement* or *slander.* Both are examples of calumny. In any case, when one disparages or slanders, he takes away someone's fame. For this reason, to defame or dishonor is to wound a person in himself: it damages his dignity. Calumny converts a worthy person into an undignified person who will be wrongly judged by the society in which he lives. Consequently, calumny is a sin against charity and against justice.

The sin of calumny is more or less serious depending on the importance of the object of the slanderous lie and also on the evils caused to the victim.

Detraction

To detract from a person's good reputation is to declare the defects or faults of another without valid reason to a person who did not know them. It is allowed to reveal the faults of another only in situations when an evil could befall another person or grave harm could come to society.

Rash Judgment

It is the interior or exterior judgment made about the reputation of a person, without sufficient reason, with which one attributes a moral defect to his neighbor.

SECTION FOUR

Reference for "Crystal Clear"

The *Catechism of the Catholic Church* states: "Conscience is a judgment of reason whereby the human person recognizes the moral quality of a concrete act that he is going to perform, is in the process of performing, or has already completed" (§1778). The conscience serves two main purposes: to help an individual to understand moral truth so as to direct his or her life according to it; and to help an individual integrate every area of life with his or her commitment of faith (see *Our Sunday Visitor's Encyclopedia of Catholic Doctrine*, entry by Patrick Lee, p. 136).

Reference for "Self-Knowledge: A Necessity for Holiness"

Conscience Formation

In *Our Sunday Visitor's Encyclopedia of Catholic Doctrine*, Patrick Lee gives five guidelines to properly forming the conscience (pp. 136-137):

- First of all, we should commit ourselves to growing in moral wisdom and to discerning, with God's grace, the moral truth concerning every aspect of our life.

- Second, we should pray, asking the Father to send us the Holy Spirit for wisdom and prudence (cf. James 1:5-6).

- Third, we should strive to appropriate personally the truth of the Gospel. Our awareness of basic moral truths, of the possibilities open to us, and of the application of moral truths to our own situation, will grow to the extent we become more virtuous, that is, to the extent we integrate every aspect of ourselves with our commitment of faith to cooperate with Jesus in redemption and to building up the kingdom. The more our intellect, emotions, and imagination are integrated with the commitment of faith, the more we are able easily to discern what is truly morally good — both in general and also in particular situations.

- We should often ask for advice. Not because only the more educated are capable of knowing moral truth, but because all of us can easily fall into self-deception and rationalization, while consulting a sound advisor can help avoid such problems.

- Church teaching should not be just one factor among others to be considered; it should be primary in the formation of one's conscience. . . . A consistent Catholic, then, does not look on the Church's moral teaching as if it were a burden. . . .

The consistent Catholic sees the Church's teaching as a precious source of light and as the primary guide for forming his conscience.

Erroneous Conscience

Because conscience is a judgment about the rightness or wrongness of specific actions, it is possible that it may be mistaken. However, it matters how it came to be mistaken. A person may or may not be at fault. When a conscience has been formed improperly it is called an "erroneous conscience." There are two kinds of poorly formed consciences. The first is called an "inculpably erroneous conscience" (also called invincible ignorance). Writing in *Our Moral Life in Christ*, Aurelio Fernandez and James Socias define an inculpably erroneous conscience as "ignorance of what is required by the moral law that is not the fault of the person acting. He has no reasonable way to know the truth. He who acts with invincible ignorance does not sin, *if he has taken the necessary and reasonable steps to learn what is permitted and prohibited*" (p. 73, emphasis added).

The second type of poorly formed conscience is called "culpably erroneous conscience" (also called vincible ignorance). Aurelio and Socias define this type of conscience as "ignorance of the truth which results from a person's failure to find out what is required of him. It is important to note here that this failure can be either willful (as in the case of a person who knows that he is in error but refuses to take the necessary steps to find out the truth) or the result of neglect (a failure to discover the truth because of laziness or disinterest). To act with vincible ignorance is to risk committing a sin" (p. 73).

Several factors can contribute to a culpably erroneous conscience. They are: habitual sin, rationalization, individualistic notion of conscience, rejection of the Church's authority and her teaching, and lack of conversion and charity.

Reference for "Know Thyself: The Examination of Conscience"

How to Make an Examination of Conscience

St. Teresa of Ávila says there is no progress in the spiritual life without self-knowledge. But self-knowledge is not easy to attain. First of all, by our very nature, we are poor self-observers. Our faults often elude us and the real motivations for our actions frequently remain hidden. This spiritual blindness makes it difficult to judge our motives, intentions, or attitudes accurately. Secondly, even when we are able to identify an interior disposition of the heart and we discover it does not conform to God's will, our initial inclination is to justify it, rationalize it, or excuse it. But, because an interior movement of the heart motivates each exterior action, we must enter upon the road to self-knowledge, as St. Teresa advises, if we are going to grow in holiness.

To gain self-knowledge, perhaps the most useful practice is an examination of conscience. Through an examination of conscience we begin to develop the spiritual eyes of our soul so that we "may judge what is God's will, what is good, pleasing and perfect" (Romans 12:2). An examination of conscience helps us in two specific ways. First, it helps us to see our sins and faults more clearly, to evaluate them according to culpability and motive, and to tame them through the grace of obedience. Secondly, an examination of conscience helps us to make progress in virtuous living. It shows us the areas where we are cooperating with the grace of God and gives us the encouragement we need to bring all areas of our lives into faithful harmony to God's will. In this way, we grow in courage, strength, perseverance, and fortitude.

How, then, do we make a good examination of conscience? The general examination of conscience reviews all of the events of the day and is very useful in giving us an overview of our thoughts, words, and deeds, and to what extent they have conformed to the will of God. Father Adolphe Tanquerey, S.S., D.D., in his classic work, *The Spiritual Life*, recommends the following method for a daily examination of conscience:

1. Because we need the assistance of God to be honest with ourselves and to illuminate our hearts to see clearly, our examination of conscience should always begin with a prayer to the Holy Spirit, asking Him to give us the grace to make our time of examination fruitful and productive.

2. Next, we must bring Jesus before us as the "Divine Model" by Whom we judge all of our actions, thoughts, words, and interior dispositions. Father Tanquerey cautions us not to be dismayed by the chasm between ourselves and Jesus, for He is the Healer of our souls.

3. Then, we begin to evaluate our external actions, and our interior motivations for them. For example, if we have been uncharitable toward our neighbor, was it because of thoughtlessness, jealousy, a desire to sound witty or charming? Then, we determine the morality of the action and our responsibility for it. "Was my behavior willful? Did I knowingly intend to be rude, hateful, or angry? Did I want to be malicious or did I put my foot in my mouth? Did I act with full consent? Was I co-

erced in some way?" All should be evaluated against the standard of Sacred Scripture, the Ten Commandments, and the teachings of the Church.

4. Finally, with true sorrow and genuine repentance, we ask God to forgive us, we ask Him to give us the grace to reform, and we ask God for the grace to live out our repentance by avoiding sin and temptation.

Reference for "Know Thyself: The Particular Examine"

The Particular Examination of Conscience

The purpose of a particular examination of conscience is to give us a "snapshot perspective" of one specific area in which we are trying to make spiritual progress. It may focus upon a sin we are working to eliminate, a fault we are trying to correct, or a virtue we are striving to cultivate. A particular examine is a great way to gain encouragement as we journey toward holiness because it allows us to see our progress on a regular basis. In fact, St. Ignatius of Loyola believed that the particular examine is even more beneficial than the general examine. He gives us rules for choosing the subject of our particular examine and the method for doing it.

How to choose the focus of a particular examine:

1. We must attack our *predominant fault.* Some of us might be able to easily identify the fault that is our greatest hindrance to spiritual progress. For others, this may be difficult — either because of our own inability to judge, or because we have several faults which seem to exert equally negative effects. For this reason, I personally recommend that we ask God to show us clearly what fault He would have us work on at a given time. By taking this course of action, we can then be assured He will give us the grace to overcome it!

2. Once we have determined which fault we are to work on, we attack its *outward manifestations,* doing away with whatever behavior might offend or scandalize others. (For example, we may discover our predominant fault is one of selfishness. Its outward manifestation may be a miserly attitude toward material possessions or toward our time or talents. Our job is to do away with selfish behavior. As we rid ourselves of the offending weakness, we then strengthen ourselves by practicing the opposite virtue. In our example, we would practice generosity with our time, talent, and treasure.)

3. Once we have begun to attack the outward manifestations of our fault, St. Ignatius recommends we move without delay to identify the *hidden cause of that fault*. What is it that causes me to think, act, or say what I do? Once the hidden motivation for our actions is exposed, we must then surrender it to the Lord, asking Him to heal us in that area of weakness and to set us free.

St. Ignatius advises that we engage ourselves in two particular examines throughout the day. This consistent and routine evaluation helps us to make real spiritual progress. He recommends that upon waking up in the morning, we remind ourselves of the sin, fault, or virtue we are working on. Then, at noontime, we review our morning in light of it. To what extent have I given in to temptation and to what extent have I acted with virtue? At suppertime, we evaluate our progress once again, looking at the afternoon hours. I suggest that we further mark our progress for the hours between the evening meal and retiring for the night. Then we can truly thank God in our nighttime prayers for His grace throughout the day.

Reference for "The Gravity of Sin"

(The following is taken from *Our Moral Life in Christ*.)

Mortal Sin

"*Mortal sin* is a grave offense against God that destroys our relationship with him by severing us from his divine love. Mortal sin is 'something grave and disordered'" (*VS*, § 70). This relationship can be restored through reconciliation.

Moral theology lists three conditions for mortal sin:

1. Grave matter "is specified by the Ten Commandments" (CCC, § 1858), that is, it must be something serious.

2. Full knowledge "presupposes knowledge of the sinful character of the act, of its opposition to God's law" (CCC, § 1859).

3. Complete consent "implies a consent sufficiently deliberate to be a personal choice" (CCC, § 1859). It is enough that one has done a prohibited thing, and he has done it deliberately.

If these three conditions are not met, no mortal sin is committed (cf. *VS*, § 70). Consequently, there is no such thing as committing a sin "by surprise"; however, sin can occur even though one does not want to offend God.

Venial Sin

"*Venial sin* offends the love of God. While it does not separate man from God, it weakens our relationship with him" (ibid.). The *Catechism of the Catholic*

Church says this about venial sin: "One commits *venial sin* when, in a less serious matter, he does not observe the standard prescribed by the moral law, or when he disobeys the moral law in a grave matter, but without full knowledge or without complete consent" (§ 1862). The *Catechism* lists the following as the effects of venial sin: "Venial sin weakens charity; it manifests a disordered affection for created goods; it impedes the soul's progress in the exercise of the virtues and the practice of the moral good; it merits temporal punishment. Deliberate and unrepented venial sin disposes us little by little to commit mortal sin. However, venial sin does not set us in direct opposition to the will and friendship of God; it does not break covenant with God. With God's grace it is humanly reparable. "Venial sin does not deprive the sinner of sanctifying grace, friendship with God, charity, and consequently eternal happiness" (§ 1863, and quoting John Paul II, *RP* 17 § 9).

Reference for "Confession: The Sacrament of Mercy and Healing"

Benefits of Frequent Confession

(The following is taken from *Mystici Corporis Christi*, § 88, Pope Pius XII, 1943.)

Pope Pius XII lists the following as the benefits to frequent confession: "Genuine self-knowledge is increased, Christian humility grows, bad habits are corrected, spiritual neglect and tepidity are resisted, the conscience is purified, the will strengthened, a salutary self-control is attained, and grace is increased in virtue of the Sacrament itself."

Reference for "The Peril of Lukewarmness"

Our Sunday Visitor's Encyclopedia of Catholic Doctrine outlines the following as a hierarchy of movement away from God (p. 268).

A Ladder to Hatred of God

- *Indifference* — stems from overlooking God's charity and ignoring His unlimited power and mercy.
- *Ingratitude* — is born of the mental sloth and unenlightened selfishness that look upon God's gifts as entitlements.
- *Lukewarmness* — arises from contradictory allegiances and a fearful spirit of calculation in the face of both divine rewards and demands.
- *Acedia* — "or spiritual sloth goes so far as to refuse the joy that comes from God and to be repelled by divine goodness" (CCC, § 2094).
- *Hatred of God* — results from proud rebellion against God's sovereignty and providence; it denies God's goodness and presumes to curse Him for impinging on one's life, for outlawing sin and meting out punishments.

Reference for "The Peril of Worldly Attachments"

How to Cultivate a Spirit of Detachment

(The following is taken from *Full of Grace: Women and the Abundant Life*.)

To cultivate a spirit of detachment, we should critically appraise our wants and desires, our thoughts and our deeds, in light of the Holy Spirit and God's holy will. Asking some hard questions will encourage us to let go of those things that are spiritually harmful and cling to those things that will help us to deepen our relationship with God.

- *Is there anything to which I have an inordinate attachment?* What is my attitude toward my job or career? Toward food and drink? Toward gambling and shopping, housecleaning and social functions?
- *Do I practice charity through tithing, almsgiving, and generosity with my time and talent?* Do I spend some time in volunteer work, freely giving of my gifts and abilities to build up the kingdom of God through service? Do I give of my treasure to those who need it — organizations or individuals? When I give, is my attitude one of cheerfulness and gratitude, or is it grudging?
- *Do the things I take in through my senses lead me closer to God or away from Him?* What do I watch on tele-

vision? What do I read? What kind of movies do I attend? How do I spend my free time? Do I have a problem with pornography? Do I dress modestly? Am I involved in any immoral relationships? Is my marriage a chaste one?

- *How do I stand on the issue of obedience?* Do I accept what I am told to do by employers, heads of committees, my parish priest, my spouse, as commands coming from God Himself — to the extent that their orders do not conflict with God's standards? Do I respond with openness of heart or with grumbling? Do I look for God's will when making important decisions in my life, or do I rush ahead with my own plans? Do I practice docility of spirit, or am I quick to fight for my own way?

Reference for "The Peril of Self-Indulgence"

The Training of the Will
(The following is taken from *The Spiritual Life*.)

812 — "In order to effect the right education of the will, we must render it supple enough to obey God in all things and strong enough to control the body and the sensitive appetites. To attain this end, obstacles must be removed and positive means employed.

A. The chief obstacles are: a) from within: 1) Lack of reflection: we do not reflect before acting and follow the impulse of the moment, passion, routine, caprice. We must take thought before acting and ask ourselves what God demands of us. 2) Over-eagerness, which, producing too great a strain, depletes the energies of body and soul to no purpose, and often causes us to stray in the direction of evil. We need self-possession and self-restraint even in doing good, so that we may start up a lasting fire rather than a darting flame. 3) Indifference, indecision, sloth, lack of moral stamina, which paralyze or atrophy our will-power. We must, then, strengthen our convictions and build up our energies. 4) The fear of failure, or lack of confidence, an attitude which notably weakens our power. We must, therefore, remind ourselves that, with God's help, we are sure of attaining good results.

813—b) To these interior obstacles are added others coming from without: 1) human respect, which makes us slaves of other men and causes us to stand in fear of their criticisms or their mockery. This is combated by realizing that what matters is not man's judgment, always liable to error, but the ever-wise and infallible judgment of God; 2) bad example, which draws us all the more easily as it is in accord with the tendency of our nature. We must remem-

Divine Healer of souls there is no incurable wound, no incurable illness.

816—c) In the last analysis it is upon the grace of God that we must learn to rely. If we beg for it with humility and confidence, it will never be refused to us, and with it we are invincible.

꧁ꙮꙮꙮꙮꙮꙮ꧂

Reference for "Faithful and True"

Seven Criteria for Discerning God's Will

(The following is taken from *Full of Grace: Women and the Abundant Life*.)

Obedience to Inspirations of Grace and the Promptings of the Holy Spirit

Our call as women is to live out our femininity authentically . . . and in so doing to become the healers of the world. To accomplish this mission through us, God desires to use us as messengers of His Good News. As a result, He often gives us inspirations, promptings, and interior urges which encourage us toward charitable acts or apostolic works. Occasionally, He will inspire us to do an extraordinary act of service in His name. When we heed these promptings, they become moments of grace for us and others. . . . However, it is important for us to discern the origin and cause of an idea or thought, lest we be the victim of our own enthusiasm, passion, or imagination — or, worse yet, a delusion of the Evil One. How, then, do we know if a prompting is from God?

Generally speaking, if the prompting conforms with the ordinary acts of charity for people in our state of life who are attempting to live a life of holiness, and if there is nothing immoral or questionable about the action, we should carry it out with gratitude that God has asked us to serve Him in this way. If, however, the prompting is out of the ordinary and is potentially life-changing in scope, we should put it to the test by evaluating it against several criteria.

First of all, is it fully in line with Sacred Scripture, the Ten Commandments, and the teachings of the Church? There is no contradiction in God — He will never go against His own precepts. If a particular action is in opposition to Sacred Scripture, it is not of God. If it goes against one of the commandments, it is not of God. If it opposes a teaching of the Church, it is not of God. If it is an uncharitable act, it is not of God. If it opposes the natural law, it is not of God. If it violates *legitimate* civil authority, it is not of God.

Secondly, is the prompting proceeding from virtue or the flesh? Another way to ask this question is, "What is my motivation?" If the desire flows from selfish gain, pride, or ostentation, the chances are very good that this is a prompting from the flesh rather than from the Spirit of God. However, if we can honestly answer that the motivation stems from the virtue of charity and love of God, then we can feel safe that our intention is honorable.

Third, has this prompting been confirmed in other ways?
God wants us to be assured of His call. He does not want us to suffer from confusion, dismay, or uncertainty. Therefore, He confirms His will for us in a variety of ways. Often, the very prompting we are experiencing will be suggested to us by another. Occasionally, someone will speak the words to us directly. And, at other times, through the normal course of conversation, a homily at Mass, a comment on the radio or television, we will recognize God's voice. God also uses Scripture to confirm His word to us. In reading a passage, the words will seem to jump off the page or they will burn in our heart long after we close the Bible. Still another way that God speaks to us is through the events of the day. Occurrences happen that seem to fit perfectly with the word we are receiving in our hearts.

Has the prompting withstood the test of time? Sometimes our enthusiasm pushes us to a decision before we have taken the time to adequately evaluate it. However, God does not take away His will for us. If we have sensed an inspiration for some time and it is valid in all other areas, we should take the prompting seriously.

Am I going through an emotionally difficult time or am I suffering from mental instability? If I am going through a difficult time emotionally — because of a serious illness, the death of a loved one, a serious financial reversal, a separation or divorce, a major disappointment or setback — or if I am suffering a mental illness or disorder that is not being treated, it is unlikely that the prompting I am hearing is coming from God. God's desire for us at times like these is to be healed by Him, most likely through others — doctors, pastors, counselors, spiritual directors. All major decisions should be delayed, if at all possible, until we are well.

Have I sought the counsel of others? Few people are in the position to make major decisions on their own; even if a person *is* in this position, it is not usually wise. For those in religious life, the guidance and permission of superiors, provincials, or bishops must be sought and obtained. Those who are married must reach agreement with their spouses, carefully considering the effects of the decision on family members. However, God often asks us to make sacrifices, and the appearance of a sacrifice should not be cause for a negative decision.

Spiritual direction is absolutely necessary when making life-changing decisions, although we should be able to judge ordinary promptings by the above criteria.

Is the supposed prompting or inspiration of grace in conformity to our state in life? We must weigh the promptings we receive against our state in life. If we sense that God is asking us to participate in certain activities, go into a particular ministry, or become a member of a certain apostolate, it will not take away from the obligations of our life in other areas. There may be sacrifice, as previously mentioned, but there will not be conflict. If there is, we must look at the inspiration with greater scrutiny. If the prompting is of God and there appears to be an obstacle or block, our attitude of heart has to be one of patient endurance — all will come to pass in His time.

Reference for "A Heart Open to All"

(The following is taken from *Our Sunday Visitor's Encyclopedia of Catholic Doctrine*, entry by Robert Royal, pp. 556, 559.)

Racism

The term "racism" covers a variety of attitudes that discriminate against people on the basis of real or imagined physical characteristics. It presumes that the human race is easily categorizable into racial types and that those types regularly display differences in intelligence or behavior. In the modern world, racism has often led to unequal treatment of people who are citizens of the same country. Segregation in the United States and apartheid in South Africa were two such cases. As such, racism is unjust, offends deeply against the equality of all people before God, and is "contrary to God's intent" (Vatican Council II, *Pastoral Constitution on the Church in the Modern World, Gaudium et Spes*, § 29).

It is important, however, to distinguish between the kind of in-group and out-group feeling that anthropologists and sociologists have found to be a feature of all human communities, and racism proper. Most human beings tend to associate with people they see as similar to themselves, whether the similarity stems from social position, religion, ethnic background, or custom. In some circumstances, people also see racial differences as constituting groups. In itself, this is not necessarily sinful or wrong. But racial self-grouping, like other forms of grouping, runs the risk of regarding those outside the group as not just different or alien, but as morally or socially inferior. When that judgment unjustly results in harmful discrimination toward individuals or whole groups on the basis of assumed racial inequalities, it becomes a serious evil. . . .

Our shared equality before God does not mean we will all show equal success in society, nor that all groups will have proportionate representation in every sector of the work and educational forces. But racism is something other than an assertion of natural human differences in ability. Racism denies that there are universally common human traits and purposes. It represents an extreme form of scientism, in that it makes certain tendencies inherited in our bodies determinative of other human factors such as will, education, intelligence, and soul. It is also an extreme form of historicism, in that it suggests different races will have different, and simply incommensurable, morals, religions, and mentalities. Majority racism has sometimes given rise to minority racism, whereby previously oppressed groups assert the superior or uncriticizable value of their own culture and roots. All of this clearly tends to a fragmenting of the human species and a denial of a common human nature given to us by God across time, space, culture, and genetic endowment.

By its very nature, Catholicism is a religion instructed by its founder, Jesus Christ, to go forth and make disciples of *all* nations (Matthew 28:19). No one is or can be excluded from God's universal love and redemptive intent. Furthermore, Catholics must not only look at all human beings as ultimately destined for God but must see all as coming from God, their Creator and common Father. Racism profoundly denies both the origin and end of human life as these are revealed in the Bible.

Reference for "Love for All Eternity"

(The following is taken from Vatican Council II, *Lumen Gentium*, § 61-62.)

Thus, in a wholly singular way she cooperated by her obedience, faith, hope and burning charity in the work of the Savior in restoring supernatural life to souls. For this reason she is mother to us in the order of grace.

This motherhood of Mary in the order of grace continues uninterruptedly from the consent which she loyally gave at the Annunciation and which she sustained without wavering beneath the cross, until the eternal fulfillment of all the elect.

SECTION SEVEN

Reference for "Transforming Deeds"

(The following is taken from *The Autobiography of St. Thérèse of Lisieux, The Story of a Soul*.)

Formerly one of our nuns managed to irritate me whatever she did or said. The devil was mixed up in it, for it was certainly he who made me see so many disagreeable traits in her. As I did not want to give way to my natural dislike for her, I told myself that charity should not only be a matter of feeling but should show itself in deeds. So I set myself to do for this sister just what I should have done for someone I loved most dearly. Every time I met her, I prayed for her and offered God all her virtues and her merits. I was sure this would greatly delight Jesus. . . .

I did not remain content with praying a lot for this nun who caused me so much disturbance. I tried to do as many things for her as I could, and whenever I was tempted to speak unpleasantly to her, I made myself give her a pleasant smile and tried to change the subject. . . .

When I was violently tempted by the devil and if I could slip away without her seeing my inner struggle, I would flee like a soldier deserting the battlefield. And after all this she asked me one day with a beaming face: "Sister *Thérèse*, will you please tell me what attracts you so much to me? You give me such a charming smile whenever we meet." Ah, it was Jesus hidden in the depth of her soul who attracted me, Jesus who makes the bitterest things sweet.

Reference for "Blossoms of a Fruitful Effort"

(The following is taken from *My Spirit Rejoices*, by Elisabeth Leseur.)

Great and holy ideas and profound convictions often reach souls only through the personal charm and attraction of those who present them. "By their fruits you shall know them," our Savior has said — by the fruits of devotion, charity, and radiant faith, and also by those flowers that first strike the eye and precede the fruit; those flowers are called sweetness, charm, nobility and exterior distinction of manners and ways, serenity, equanimity, friendliness, smiles, and simplicity.

Bibliography

Alberione, Very Rev. James, S.S.P., S.T.D., *Woman: Her Influence and Zeal*, Milwaukee, Wisc., St. Paul Editions, 1964.

Attwater, Donald, General Editor, *A Catholic Dictionary*, Rockford, Ill., Tan Books and Publishers, Inc., 1997.

Belligio, Sister Concetta, D.S.P., Editor, *Real Women*, San Francisco, Calif., Ignatius Press, 1994.

Benkovic, Johnnette, *Full of Grace: Women and the Abundant Life*, Ann Arbor, Mich., Servant Publications, 1998.

Bouyer, Louis, *Introduction to Spirituality*, Translated by Mary Perkins Ryan, Tournai, Belgium, Desclee & Company, 1961.

Bouyer, Louis, *Woman in the Church*, Translated by Marilyn Teichert, San Francisco, Calif., Ignatius Press, 1984.

Catechism of the Catholic Church, Second Edition, United States Catholic Conference, Inc. (Washington, D.C.) — Libreria Editrice Vaticana (Vatican City, Rome, Italy), 1994, 1997.

Day, Dorothy, *From Union Square to Rome*, Silver Springs, Md., Preservation, Dorothy Day Library on the Web at www.catholicworker.org/dorothyday/.

Fernandez, Aurelio and James Socias, *Our Moral Life in Christ*, Princeton, N.J., Scepter Publishers, Inc., 1997.

Fernandez, Francis, *In Conversation with God, Vol. 2*, London, England, Scepter, 1997.

Johnston, Francis W., Selected and Arranged By, *The Voices of the Saints*, Rockford, Ill., Tan Books and Publishers, Inc., 1986.

Leseur, Elisabeth, *My Spirit Rejoices*, Manchester, N.H., Sophia Institute Press, 1996.

The Liturgy of the Hours, Vol. III, New York, N.Y., Catholic Book Publishing Co., 1975.

McInerny, Ralph, Editor, *The Catholic Woman (Papers Presented at a Conference Sponsored by the Wethersfield Institute)*, San Francisco, Calif., Ignatius Press, 1991.

Moll, Helmut, Editor, *The Church and Women: A Compendium*, San Francisco, Calif., Ignatius Press, 1988.

The Monks of Solesmes, Selected and Arranged By, *The Woman in the Modern World*, Boston, Mass., St. Paul Editions, 1959 ("Allocution to Italian Women," Pope Pius XII, October 31, 1945).

Mother Teresa of Calcutta, *Heart of Joy: The Transforming Power of Self-Giving*, Ann Arbor, Mich., Servant Publications, 1987.

Shaw, Russell, Editor, *Our Sunday Visitor's Encyclopedia of Catholic Doctrine*, Huntington, Ind., Our Sunday Visitor, 1997.

Stein, Edith, *The Collected Works of Edith Stein, Vol. II, "Essays on Woman,"* Translated by Freda Mary Oben, Ph.D., Washington, D.C., ICS Publications, 1987.

Stern, Anthony, M.D., *Everything Starts from Prayer: Mother Teresa's Meditations on Spiritual Life for People of All Faiths*, Ashland, Ore., White Cloud Press, 1998.

Tanquerey, Very Rev. Adolphe, S.S., D.D., *The Spiritual Life: A Treatise on Ascetical and Mystical Theology*, Translated by Rev. Herman Branderis, S.S., A.M., Tournai, Belgium, Desclee & Company, 1930.

Teresa of Ávila, *The Life of Saint Teresa of Ávila By Herself*, Translated by J. M. Cohen, London, England, Penguin Classics, 1957.

Teresa of Ávila, *The Way of Perfection*, Translated by E. Allison Peers, New York, N.Y., Image Books, Doubleday, 1991.

Thérèse of Lisieux, *The Autobiography of St. Thérèse of Lisieux: The Story of a Soul*, Translated by John Beevers, Garden City, N.Y., Image Books, Doubleday, 1957.

Thoughts of Saint Thérèse, Translated from the French *Pensées* by an Irish Carmelite, Rockford, Ill., Tan Books and Publishers, Inc., 1988.

von le Fort, Gertrud, *The Eternal Woman*, Translated by Placid Jordon, O.S.B., Milwaukee, Wisc., The Bruce Publishing Company, 1961.

Catholic Church Documents

Closing Speeches, Vatican Council II, *To Women*, read by Leon Cardinal Duval of Algiers, Algeria, assisted by Julius Cardinal Doepfner of Munich, Germany, and Raul Cardinal Silva of Santiago, Chile, December 8, 1965, printed by the Daughters of St. Paul, Boston, Mass.

Mother of the Redeemer, Pope John Paul II, March 25, 1987.

Reconciliatio et Paenitentia, Pope John Paul II, December 2, 1984.

Salvifici Doloris, Pope John Paul II, February 11, 1984.